MW01235187

The
BIG
Dictionary

First Edition
January 2001

Lorren Daro Productions
Cobb Mountain, California

www.BIGdictionary.com

The BIG Dictionary
Copyright ©2001 by Lorren Daro
All Rights Reserved

ISBN: 0-9706608-0-4

Manufactured in the U.S.A.
by KNI, Inc., Anaheim, California

Lorren Daro Productions
P.O. Box 9
Cobb, CA 95426

On the Internet:
www.BIGdictionary.com

Cover Design: Christine Beebe

Typesetting: Tamara Kestrel

=A=

abandon lack of control; recklessness

abase to cause to feel ashamed or unimportant

abashed embarrassed

abate to become less strong

abbreviate to shorten

abdicate to give up a high office or position of power

abduct to take away by force; kidnap

aberration an unusual and temporary change

abet to help or encourage someone to do something wrong

abeyance temporary suspension

abhor to hate very strongly; detest

abide to endure willingly

abject in a miserable condition; deserving no respect

abjure to swear to avoid or discontinue

ablution the act of washing oneself

abnegate to renounce or relinquish

abode one's home

abolish to do away with

abominable hateful

abominate to hate

aboriginal having existed in a place from the beginning

aborning being born

abort to prevent from developing any further; to end a pregnancy

abound to exist in large numbers

abrade to wear away by rubbing

abreast side by side

abridge to shorten a book, speech, etc.

abrogate to officially end a law, agreement, etc.

abscond to go away secretly and hide, esp. to avoid arrest

absentee not present; not in residence

absolution the formal act of being forgiven for one's sins

absolve to officially free someone of guilt or responsibility for error

abstain to keep oneself from doing something pleasurable

abstemious deliberately restraining oneself, as from eating or drinking

abstinence the act of refraining from having sex

abstract existing as an idea or quality rather than as an object

abstruse difficult to understand

abusive using rude and offensive language or physical abuse

abut to border on

abysmal awful; terrible

abyss a dark, bottomless pit

academe or **academia** the world of colleges and universities

academic related to studying and learning

a cappella sung without musical accompaniment

accede to agree to

accelerate to increase in speed

accentuate to emphasize

accessible easily reached or understood

acclaim public approval or praise

acclimate or **acclimatize** to adapt to a new environment or situation

acclivity an upward slope

accolade an expression of praise

accommodate to provide what someone needs

accompany to go with someone or something

accomplice one who helps another to do something wrong; a partner in crime

accord agreement

accost to boldly approach and speak to a stranger

2

accountable   completely responsible

accoutrements or **accouterments**   the equipment needed for a particular purpose

accretion   gradual buildup or growth

accrue   to increase gradually

accursed   very annoying

accusatory   placing blame

accustom   to make oneself used to something

acerbic   harsh; sharp; biting

acetic   having the properties of vinegar

Achilles' heel   a weak point or vulnerable place

acidulous   sour; sharp

acknowledge   to accept or recognize something as true; to show that you have received something

acme   the highest point of achievement

acolyte   a follower or helper, esp. an altar attendant in some religious ceremonies

acoustic   relating to sound or hearing

acquiesce   to agree to something, usually unwillingly

acquisitive   greedily seeking to acquire things

acquit   (in law) to decide that someone is not guilty of a crime

acrid   strongly irritating to the nose or throat

acrimonious   bitter and angry

acronym   a word formed from the first letter of each word in a phrase

acrophobia   fear of heights

actualize   to make happen or take place

actuary   a person who calculates rates for insurance companies

actuate   to move to act or put into action

acuity   sharpness and accuracy, as of eyesight or thought

acumen   skill in making judgments or decisions

acupuncture a Chinese medical practice that treats diseases and pain by inserting needles at specific sites on the body

acute severe or intense, as pain; sharp and accurate, as hearing

adage a wise saying; proverb

adamant unwilling to change one's opinion; stubborn

adamantine completely unyielding; unbreakable

addendum something added, as to a book

addled mentally confused

adduce to offer as proof or explanation

adept skilled

adhere to stick firmly

ad hoc for a specific purpose

ad hominem (of an argument) directed at a person's character rather than at the issue at hand

ad infinitum without end

adipose relating to animal fat

adjacent next to; touching

adjoin to be next to or connected with

adjourn to stop a meeting, trial, etc., for a period of time

adjudge to consider or declare officially

adjudicate to act as judge

adjunct an addition or attachment to something more important

adjure to urge or advise seriously

ad lib said without advance preparation

administrate to manage or govern

admissible able to be allowed or admitted, as in a legal case

admixture something added to something else

admonish to criticize in a kindly way; to caution

adorn to add something decorative

ad nauseam to the point of disgust

adrift without direction or purpose

adroit skillful and quick

adulation excessive admiration or praise

adulterate to make something weaker or less pure by adding something else

adultery sex between a married person and someone who is not his or her spouse

adumbrate to give a faint idea or indication, esp. of something in the future

advent the arrival of something new

adventitious unexpected; unplanned

adversary an enemy

adverse going against one's interests; harmful

adversity an unlucky situation; misfortune

advisedly on purpose; deliberately

advocate (v) to propose or support an idea or cause

advocate (n) one who speaks in support of something; a lawyer

aegis protection or support

aeon or **eon** an immeasurably long period of time

aerie an eagle's nest

aerobic (of exercise) improving the body's ability to use oxygen

aesthete or **esthete** a person who fully appreciates and enjoys beauty, esp. in art

aesthetic or **esthetic** relating to the enjoyment of beauty

affable friendly and kind

affectation artificial behavior intended to impress

affected artificial; insincere

affectless uncaring; indifferent

affidavit a written legal statement swearing that something is true

affiliation a close association or relationship

affinity an attraction; a likeness or similarity

affirm to maintain that something is true; to support

affirmation the assertion that something is true

affix to attach

afflict to cause physical or mental suffering to

affluence wealth; prosperity

affront an insult

aficionado an enthusiastic fan

aforementioned mentioned earlier

afoul entangled; in conflict with

aftermath the result or consequence, as of a harmful event

agape (n) (a.GAH.pay) pure love

agape (adj) (a.GAPE) with the mouth open in surprise

agenda a list of things to be done or discussed

agglomeration a mass of many things gathered together

aggrandize to increase in power, rank, or wealth

aggravate to irritate or annoy

aggregate a total composed of loosely associated parts

aggrieved angry or hurt because of unfair treatment

aghast shocked; horrified

agility the ability to move quickly and easily

agitation great excitement or anxiety

agitprop political propaganda

agnostic one who believes that it is not possible to know whether God exists

agog excited; eager

agon a conflict or contest

agrarian related to farming

aide-de-camp a military or naval officer who assists an officer of superior rank

ajar partially open

akimbo (of the arms) with elbows bent and hands on hips

akin having similar qualities

alacrity eager promptness

albeit although

albino a person or animal born without normal skin pigment

alchemy a type of chemistry of the Middle Ages which attempted to turn other metals into gold

aleatory caused by chance or accident

alfresco in the open air

alias a false name

alienate to cause a loss of support or friendship

allay to make fears, doubts, etc., less strong

allegation a statement or accusation made without proof

allege to claim but not prove that something is true

allegiance loyalty or devotion

allegory a story, play, etc., in which the characters represent ideas or moral principles

alleviate to make pain, sorrow, etc., easier to bear

alliance a group of countries, political parties, etc., that have joined together for a shared purpose

alliteration the use of several words having the same initial sound, esp. in poetry

allocate to give or set aside for a particular purpose

allotment a portion or share granted

alloy a mixture of metals, as bronze

allude to refer to someone or something indirectly

allure attraction; charm

allusion an indirect reference

ally a friend or partner

alma mater the college or university that one attended

alms money or food given to the poor

aloft in the air; in a higher position

aloof unfriendly and distant

altercation a fight or loud argument

altruism charitable concern for the welfare of others

alumna (pl. **alumnae)** a female graduate of a college or university

alumnus (pl. **alumni)** a male graduate of a college or university

amalgam a combination or mixture

amalgamate to combine or unite

amanuensis a person employed to write down what another person says

amass to gather together a large amount, as of money

amatory relating to sexual love

ambidextrous able to use both hands equally well

ambience or **ambiance** the special quality or atmosphere of a place

ambient existing in the surrounding environment

ambiguous having more than one possible meaning; unclear

ambivalent having conflicting feelings about something; uncertain

ambrosia the food of the Greek and Roman gods; any very delicious food

ambulate to walk around

ameliorate to make a situation or condition better

amenable willing to consider or accept a suggestion

amend to change or add to a law, constitution, etc.

amends compensation for a wrong done

amenity something that adds to people's pleasure or comfort

amiable friendly and pleasant

amicable friendly; peaceable

amiss wrong; not as expected

amity friendship

amnesty a pardon for past crimes

amoral having no moral principles

amorous relating to sexual desire

amorphous having no fixed form

amortize to repay a loan in regular amounts over a period of time

amphibian an animal that lives both on land and in the water

amuck or **amok** in a wild or violent manner

anachronism something that is out of its place in time

anagram a word or phrase made by reordering the letters of another word or phrase

analgesic a drug that relieves pain

analogous similar; corresponding

analogy similarity in certain ways between two things

anarchy political and social disorder in the absence of governmental control

anathema something that is greatly hated

ancillary providing additional help or support

androgynous having both male and female features

android a robot that resembles a human being

anecdote a brief account of an incident or event

anemic lacking power or vitality; weak

anesthetic a drug that makes a person unable to feel pain

angst a feeling of great anxiety or anguish

animadversion the act of criticizing; an unfavorable comment

animism the belief that all natural things have spirits

animosity strong dislike or opposition

animus strong dislike; enmity

annals historical records

anneal to make metal or glass soft by heating and gradually cooling

annex to take possession of something, as

an area of land, esp. without permission

annihilate to destroy completely

annotate to add a brief explanation to a text

annuity a fixed amount of money paid each year

annul to declare a marriage, agreement, etc., legally void

annunciate to announce

anodyne anything that relieves pain or soothes feelings

anoint to put oil on someone in a religious ceremony; to choose someone formally

anomalous irregular; abnormal

anomaly a deviation from what is normal or usual

anomic socially isolated

anomie a feeling of unrest and isolation resulting from a lack of values

anonymous unnamed; unknown

anorexia an eating disorder marked by an abnormal fear of weight gain that results in an inability to eat

antagonism hostility; opposition

antagonist opponent; adversary

antagonize to earn the opposition or dislike of others; offend

antebellum before the war, esp. the American Civil War

antecedent a person or thing that comes before something else

antediluvian very old or old-fashioned

anthology a collection of writings by various authors

anthropoid resembling humans or apes

anthropomorphic giving human form or qualities to something that is not human

antic funny; whimsical; odd

Antichrist the New Testament adversary of Christ; an opponent or denier of Christ or Christianity

anticlimax a disappointingly weak result

or conclusion

antidote   something that prevents or acts against harmful effect

antipathy   strong dislike or opposition

antipode   the exact opposite

antiquated   old-fashioned

antiquity   ancient times, esp. before the Middle Ages

antithesis   the exact opposite

antonym   a word that means the opposite of another word

apartheid   a political system that requires racial separation

apathy   lack of interest or energy; indifference

ape   to imitate badly

aperçu   a quick look at something

aperture   a small or narrow opening

apex   the highest point

aphorism   a short saying that expresses a general truth

apiary   a place where bees are kept

aplomb   confidence and poise

apocalypse   the end of the world

apocryphal   (of a story) often told but probably not true

apogee   the highest point

apolitical   not involved with political matters

apologia   a formal defense of a belief or system

apoplexy   a stroke or fit

apostate   one who has abandoned a religious faith or a political party

apostle   a strong supporter or believer

apothecary   formerly, a pharmacist

apotheosis   the ideal example

appalling   shocking; extremely bad

apparition   a ghost

appease   to calm or satisfy by yielding what is demanded

appellate   (of a court) having the power to

change the decision of a lower court

appellation a name or title

append to add or attach

appertain to belong to, esp. officially

applicable able to be applied; appropriate

apportion to share among several persons or things

appose to place next to

apposite suitable; right

appraise to estimate the quality or value of something

apprehend to understand completely; to capture or arrest

apprehensive anxious; fearful

apprise to tell; inform

approachable easy to talk to; friendly

approbation approval; praise

appropriate (adj) suitable for a particular situation

appropriate (v) to set apart or take for a particular use

approximate (adj) almost exact or accurate

approximate (v) to be almost the same as

appurtenance an additional feature or possession

a priori presupposed by experience; formed or conceived beforehand

apropos suitable; relevant

aptitude natural ability or skill

aptness suitability for a particular occasion

aquiline (of a nose) curved like an eagle's beak

arable (of land) suitable for growing crops

arbiter a person having the power to make a judgment

arbitrary based on chance or personal power rather than reason

arbitrate to serve as a judge in a dispute

arboreal relating to or living in trees

arcane known only by a few special people; secret; obscure

arch coy; crafty; sly

archaic out-of-date; ancient

archetype an original model or typical example

archive a place where historical records are kept

ardent strongly enthusiastic; eager

ardor great warmth or enthusiasm

arduous difficult and tiring

argot the special vocabulary of a particular group

aria a song sung by one person in an opera

arid very dry

armada a large fleet of ships

Armageddon in the New Testament, a final war between good and evil; an event of great destruction

aromatic having a strong, pleasant smell

arraign to formally call into a court of law to answer a charge

array (n) an orderly arrangement

array (v) to display or dress up

arrears the state of being in debt

arresting attracting attention or interest; striking

arrhythmia any disturbance in heartbeat rhythm

arriviste a person who is new to social status or wealth

arrogance self-importance; haughtiness

arrogate to take something without right

artful clever, skillful, cunning

articulate (adj) able to express oneself clearly

articulate (v) to express in words

artifact an object made by a person, as a tool

artifice deception; trickery

artisan a person skilled in a trade; craftsman

artless natural, simple, uncontrived

ascend to go or move upward; rise

ascendancy or **ascendency** controlling power or influence

ascertain to make certain; discover

ascetic practicing severe self-denial

ascribe to give as a reason for; attribute

ashen the color of ashes

asinine extremely stupid

askance with disapproval or suspicion

askew not straight or level

asocial rejecting social interaction

aspect a particular feature or point of view

asperity harshness of tone or manner; severity

aspersion a damaging remark; slur

asphyxiate to suffocate

aspiration a strong desire to achieve a goal or ideal

aspire to have a great ambition; desire strongly

assail to attack physically or verbally

assay to test or evaluate; to attempt

assent agreement

assert to state forcefully

assess to evaluate

assiduous marked by careful attention and hard work

assimilate to take in or become similar to

assonance repeated use of a vowel in several words, esp. in poetry

assuage to calm, as fear; to satisfy, as hunger

assumption something accepted as true without proof

asunder broken into pieces

assure to give confidence to; convince

asunder widely separated into parts

astigmatism a fault in the lens of the eye that causes improper focusing

14

astral relating to or coming from the stars

astringent severe or bitter

astute clever and quick in judgment

asylum protection or safety

asymmetrical having two halves or parts that are not exactly the same

atavism reversion to an earlier or more primitive type

atelier a workshop or studio

atheist one who believes that God does not exist

athwart in opposition to; contrary to

atone to make up for a sin or other wrong

atrocity a very cruel or shocking action

atrophy (of a body part) to waste away; to become weaker

attenuate to make smaller or weaker

attest to say or prove that something is true

attribute (n) a quality or characteristic of a person or thing

attribute (v) to consider as the result or work of someone or something else

attrition a gradual wearing away and weakening

atypical not usual for its type

au contraire to the contrary

au courant fully informed; up-to-date

audacity insolence; rudeness

audit to examine and verify financial records; to attend a college course for no credit

augment to make larger; increase

augur to be a sign of something in the future

august inspiring reverence or admiration; of great dignity

aura a feeling or quality that characterizes a person or thing

auspices support and protection

auspicious suggesting a successful outcome or result

austere plain or bare

auteur (oh.TUR) a film director who is the chief creator of a film

authenticate to establish as being true or genuine

authoritative known to be accurate and reliable

autism a developmental disorder marked by failure to develop social abilities

autocrat one who rules with unlimited power

autodidact a person who is self-taught

automaton a person who acts in a mechanical fashion

autonomous self-governing; independent

autopsy a medical examination of a dead body to determine the cause of death

auxiliary giving assistance or support

avail use, purpose, or advantage

avant-garde new and original in style, ideas, or methods

avarice extreme greed

avatar a god incarnated in human form

aver to declare strongly; assert

averse opposed; disinclined

aversion a strong dislike

avert to prevent something bad from happening

aviary a place where birds are kept

avid extremely eager or interested

avocation one's usual employment, or something one does in addition to this, esp. as a hobby

avow to state or admit something

avuncular like an uncle; friendly and caring

awe a feeling of great admiration and respect

awry wrong; amiss

axiom a statement that is generally accepted as true

azure a bright blue color

=B=

Babbit a conventional, self-satisfied conformist

baccalaureate the bachelor's degree; the lowest degree awarded by a four-year college

bacchanal a wild, noisy party

backbite to say unkind or mean things about someone who is not present

backlog a large accumulation of unfinished work

back number something that is not current

backpedal to take back an opinion you had expressed before

backwater a place that is not influenced by new ideas and shows little growth or activity

badger to annoy or criticize someone repeatedly

badinage (bad.i.NAZH) good-natured joking

bagatelle a thing of no importance

bagnio a house of prostitution

bailiff a minor official in a courtroom

bailiwick a person's field of authority or knowledge

baksheesh a tip or bribe

balderdash nonsense

baleful evil or harmful

balk to stop and be unwilling to continue

ballast something heavy carried in the bottom of a ship to steady it; anything that steadies a person or thing

balletic like the graceful movements of ballet

ballistic relating to the firing characteristics of a missile

balm anything that soothes or heals

banal (ba.NAL) overused and boring

bandy to speak of something lightly and carelessly

bane a cause of harm or ruin; a curse

baneful causing serious harm; destructive

banish to force to go away, as from a country

banquette a long bench with an upholstered seat

banter light, playful conversation

baptism a religious ceremony in which a person is sprinkled with or dipped in water as a sign of admission to the Christian church

barb a sharply critical remark

barbarous savagely harsh or cruel

baroque (ba.ROKE) elaborately decorated; fanciful; grotesque

barrage a steady firing of large guns to protect advancing troops; a large number of complaints, questions, etc., directed at someone all at once

barrister (in England) a lawyer who is qualified to plead cases in higher courts

barter to exchange goods for other goods rather than for money; trade

baseless having no foundation in fact

baseness lack of decency or honor; immorality

bask to lie in the pleasant warmth of the sun; to take great pleasure in approval or fame

bas-relief (bah.ri.LEEF) a style of sculpture in which the shapes project only slightly from a flat background

bastardize to change something in a way that lowers its quality or value

bastille a prison

bastion a fortified place; something that defends or protects a position or belief

bate to reduce in force or intensity; lessen or diminish

bathetic overly sentimental; trite
bathos overdone sentimentality
batten to fasten down
bawdy humorously vulgar; lewd
beatific blissful
beatitude a state of extreme happiness
beau geste (boh ZHEST) a beautiful gesture
beau monde the fashionable world of high society
becalmed not moving or advancing
beckon to entice or attract
bedazzle to impress greatly
bedlam a wild scene of noisy disorder; madhouse
bedraggled wet and messy
beeline a direct course
befuddle to confuse
begrudge to give or allow with reluctance or envy
beguile to charm or delight; to deceive
behemoth something of huge size or power
behest an order or urgent request
beholden feeling indebted to someone for a favor or gift
behoove to be necessary or proper
belabor to insist on or explain something more than is necessary
belated later than expected
beleaguered beset with difficulties; harassed
belie to give a wrong or false impression of something
belittle to make someone or something seem unimportant; disparage
belles lettres fine literature
bellicose eager to fight; aggressively hostile
belligerent eager to fight or argue; hostile
bellwether a person or thing that leads or sets a trend

bemoan to express sadness or regret about something

bemused absorbed in thought; slightly confused

benchmark a standard by which others can be judged

benediction a blessing

benefactor someone who gives financial aid to a person or group

beneficent doing acts of kindness or charity

beneficiary one who benefits, as from the terms of a will

benevolent kind and helpful

benighted lacking in knowledge or morals

benign gentle and kind; (of a tumor) not malignant

benumb to make numb because of cold, shock, etc.

bequeath to hand down money or property, as by will

bequest something that is handed down in a will

berate to criticize someone angrily; scold

bereavement the loss of a loved one by death

bereft deprived of something; feeling great loss

berserk violently out of control

beseech to beg eagerly for something

beset attacked from all directions; surrounded, as by difficulties

besiege to surround with enemy forces; to harass, as with doubts

besmirch to ruin or soil, as a reputation

besotted completely in love

bespeak to suggest or show

bespoke (of clothes) made to individual order

bestial cruel or debased; inhuman

bestiality sex with an animal

bestow to present as a gift or honor

bête noire (bet.nwar) something that is greatly disliked or dreaded

betoken to be a sign of something

betrothed engaged to be married

bevy a large group or collection

bewildered confused; perplexed

bias a tendency or prejudice

bibliography a list of books and articles on a particular subject or by a specific author

bibliophile a lover of books

bibulous overly fond of alcoholic drinks

bicameral (of a legislative body) having two parts or houses

bicker to argue about unimportant things

bide to wait

bidet a small, low bathroom fixture used for washing the genital area

biennial every two years

bier a stand or frame on which a coffin is placed before burial

bifurcate to divide into two parts

bigamy the crime of being married to two people at the same time

bigotry prejudice; intolerance

bijou small, delicate ring or jewel

Bildungsroman a novel about a young person's education and development into maturity

bilious suffering from trouble with the bile or liver; cranky or irritable; (of a color) unpleasant

bilk to cheat or defraud

billow to become filled with air and swell out

binary consisting of two parts

binge a bout of excessive eating, drinking, etc.

biodegradable able to decay naturally

biomass the amount of living matter in an area

biopsy the surgical removal of tissue from

a living body for examination and
diagnosis

bipartisan involving members of two
political parties

bipartite consisting of two parts

biped an animal with two feet

bipolar referring to a mental disorder that
is marked by the alternation of manic and
depressive states

birthright a right to which one is entitled
by birth

bisexual sexually attracted to both men and
women

bistro a small cafe, bar, or nightclub

bizarre very strange and unusual; weird

blackball to prevent someone from
becoming a member of an organization or
group

black box any small, usually complex or
mysterious electronic device that is
dedicated to performing a specific
function

blackguard (BLAG.ard) a man without
principles or morals

blacklist to put someone on a list of people
to be disapproved and penalized

blanch to turn pale; (of vegetables) to
place very briefly in boiling water

blandishments words or actions intended
to persuade or flatter

blasé (blah.ZAY) showing no interest or
emotion

blasphemous religiously offensive

blasphemy the act of showing disrespect
for God or anything sacred

blatant obvious in an offensive or
shameless way

blather to talk in a foolish way

blazon to set forth or display
conspicuously

bleak cold and unfriendly; hopeless

bleary (of eyes) red and watery

blighted in a ruined or decayed condition

blind-sided unpleasantly surprised, as if hit from one's blind side

blinkered lack of understanding; obscured vision

blithe happy and unworried

blithering talking nonsense

bloated swollen, as with too much air or food

blouson a woman's garment with a close-fitting waistband that makes the fabric above it fall in loose folds over it

bloviate to speak in a lengthy and unpleasantly proud and self-important manner

blowzy or **blowsy** (of a woman) sloppy in appearance

bludgeon to hit someone repeatedly with a heavy weapon

blurb a brief, favorable description of a work, as on the jacket of a book

bluster loud, empty boasts or threats

bodacious remarkable; outstanding

bode to be a sign of something in the future

bodega a Hispanic grocery store

bodice the upper part of a dress

boggle to bewilder or confuse, as the mind

bohemian a person, as an artist or writer, who has an unconventional lifestyle

boisterous noisy and rough

Bolshevism a political system introduced in Russia in 1917

bolster to make something stronger; support

bombastic using showy or affected language in order to seem important

bona fides (BOH.na FIE.deez) authentic evidence of one's qualifications or intentions

bon ami (fem. bonne amie) good friend; lover

bonhomie good-natured friendliness: geniality

bon mot (MOH) a clever or witty remark

bon ton something regarded as fashionable or proper; high society

bon vivant (vee.VAHN) a person who lives well and has refined tastes in food and wine

boondocks a sparsely inhabited and remote rural area

boondoggle a wasteful activity of little or no value

boor a rude, inconsiderate person

boorish crude; offensive

bordello a brothel

bosom a woman's breasts

botch to spoil something by doing it poorly or carelessly

boudoir a woman's bedroom or private sitting room

bouffant full, puffed-out hair or clothing

bounder a man with no principles or morals

boundless unlimited

bountiful plentiful; abundant; generous

bourgeois typical of the middle class; caring too much about possessions and social conventions

bowdlerize to remove from a book, play, etc., parts that are considered offensive

boycott to refuse to buy certain products or deal with certain stores or organizations as a means of expressing strong disapproval

brackish (of water) slightly salty and unpleasant

braggadocio (brag.a.DOH.shee.oh) empty boasting

brahmin an aristocrat who is intellectually or socially aloof

Braille a system of raised printing for the blind

24

bravado (bra.VAH.doh) a show of bravery

brazen boldly rude or shameless

breach (n) an act of breaking a promise, law, relationship, etc.; a gap made in a wall or fortification

breach (v) to break through a fortification, or a line of enemy soldiers

breadth width; scope

brevity shortness, as of something written or said

brigand an armed robber; bandit

brio liveliness; vigor

brisk quick and energetic

bristle to show sudden anger or annoyance

brittle easily broken or snapped

broach to open up a discussion of something

broadside a strong spoken or written attack

bromide a boring, overused remark

brood to think deeply and unhappily; worry

brouhaha a lot of noise, excitement, or confusion

bruit to tell everyone, as a piece of news

brunt the full force of something difficult

brusque rude and abrupt

buccaneer an unscrupulous adventurer; a pirate

bucolic related to rural life

bugaboo something that causes worry or fear

bulimia an eating disorder marked by overeating and purging

bulwark something that protects or supports

bumptious noisily self-confident

buncombe or **bunkum** insincere talk; nonsense

bungle to do something clumsily

buoyant   able to float; cheerful
bureaucracy   a government or business in which there is excessive concentration of power in minor officials who follow complex rules
bureaucrat   an official in a bureaucracy
burgeon   to develop or grow quickly
burlesque   a comic piece of writing or acting that ridicules a serious work
burly   (of a man) large and strong
burnish   to polish
bursar   a treasurer or business officer
bush-league   inferior; second-rate
busk   to perform in the street for donations
buttress   to strengthen and support
buxom   (of a woman) large-breasted
byword   a person or thing that typifies a particular quality; a frequently used phrase

=C=

cabal a small, secret group of plotters, as against a government

cache a hidden supply, as of food or weapons

cachet (ka.SHAY) a special and distinctive quality that marks superior status

cacophony an unpleasant and loud mixture of sounds

cadaver a dead body

cadence a rhythmic flow of sound, as in poetry

cadge to borrow without intending to repay

cadre a core group of trained personnel

cagey cautious and shrewd

cajole to persuade by flattery or promises

calamity an event that causes loss and suffering; misfortune

calcify to harden or become rigid

caliber the width of the hole in the barrel of a gun; degree of competence or merit

calibrate to adjust precisely for a particular use

calisthenics gymnastic exercises

calligraphy the art of beautiful handwriting

callous unfeeling and unkind

callow immature and inexperienced

calumny a false and malicious statement; slander

camaraderie a warm feeling of friendship

cameo a brief role played by a famous actor in a film or play; profile of a head carved in a precious stone

camouflage a means of concealing something by altering or covering it

camp something amusingly outrageous or overdone

campaign an organized effort intended to achieve a particular aim

canard a false and deceptive piece of information

candid honest and direct; straightforward

candor honest and open expression, esp. about a difficult subject

cannabis the hemp plant; marijuana

canny careful and shrewd

canon a body of rules or code of laws, as in a religion; the authentic works of a writer; the formally accepted body of works within a field

canonize to declare officially to be a saint

cant language peculiar to a particular class or profession; hypocritically pious speech

cantankerous bad-tempered

canvass to visit an area to solicit opinions or votes

capacious able to hold a lot; roomy

capital (n) wealth, esp. money used to produce more wealth

capital (adj) (of a crime) punishable by death

capitulate to surrender under stated terms

capo the head of a branch of the Mafia

caprice a sudden, unpredictable change, as of behavior

capricious changing frequently and unpredictably; undependable

capsize to overturn

caption a short explanation under a picture; a subtitle in a film

captious tending to criticize or find fault

captivate to fascinate or charm

carapace the hard shell of certain animals, as a turtle

carat a unit of weight for precious stones and metals

carcass the parts left of a dead animal; the

remains of something

carcinogen a substance that causes or tends to cause cancer

carcinoma a cancerous tumor

cardinal of great importance; chief

careen to sway to one side while going forward quickly

career (n) a life's work, esp. in a profession

career (v) to go at full speed

cargo freight carried by a ship or plane

caricature an exaggerated drawing of a person; a bad or laughable example of something

carnage slaughter of large numbers of people

carnal sexual

carnivore an animal that eats meat

carouse to have a merry time, esp. while drinking

carp to criticize and complain constantly

carpe diem seize the day

carrion the decaying flesh of dead animals

carte blanche complete freedom

cartel a group of companies that join together to control prices and markets

cartography the art of making maps

cascade a small waterfall or a series of waterfalls; something that flows or falls in abundance

caste a social class, as in India

castigate to criticize severely

castrate to remove the testicles

casuistry false or dishonest reasoning

casus belli a cause of war

cataclysm a great disaster or upheaval

catalyst a person or thing that causes or speeds up an important change

catamite a boy who is in a sexual relationship with a man

cataract a clouding of the lens of the eye; a large waterfall

catarrh chronic inflammation of the mucous membrane of the respiratory tract

catatonic characterized by an abnormal lack of movement or expression

catcall a loud shout or whistle expressing disapproval

catechism a book of questions and answers about an established set of religious beliefs

categorical without exception; certain

caterwaul to make a high, wailing noise like a cat

catharsis the release of strong emotions; relief of emotional tensions

cathexis the investment of emotional energy in someone or something

catholic broad in scope; wide-ranging

caucus a closed political meeting to select candidates or determine policy

cauldron a large kettle for boiling

causality the relation between cause and effect

causative acting as a cause

cause celebre a matter, such as a legal trial, that attracts widespread public attention

caustic severely critical and hurtful

cauterize to burn a wound in order to stop bleeding or prevent infection

cavalcade a procession of people, horses, cars, etc.

cavalier thoughtless; uncaring

caveat a warning

caveat emptor let the buyer beware

cavernous having a huge open space inside

cavil to raise trivial objections

cavort to leap about playfully

cede to give up possession, as by treaty

celerity speed or quickness

celestial relating to the sky or heaven

celibate abstaining from sex, esp. for

religious reasons

censor to remove parts of books, films, etc., that are considered objectionable

censure strong criticism or disapproval

centenary the 100th anniversary

centrifugal moving in a direction away from a center or axis

centripetal moving in a direction toward a center or axis

centrist a person who supports moderate political policies

cerebral relating to the brain or the intellect; requiring mental effort

cerebration the process of thinking

cessation the act of ending or stopping

cession the act of giving away, as by treaty

cetacean belonging to an order of marine mammals, as the whales and dolphins

chafe to feel irritated; lose patience

chaff unimportant or worthless ideas

chagrin strong disappointment or annoyance, esp. that caused by a mistake or failure

chameleon a person who quickly adopts the opinions or behavior of others

chaotic in complete disorder

chaplain a member of the clergy who is responsible for the religious needs of an institution or military unit

characteristic a typical or noticeable quality of a person or thing

characterize to describe using a comparison

charade something that is clearly false or deceptive

charisma a special quality or power that enables an individual to attract and influence others

charlatan a person who falsely claims to have expert knowledge or skills

chary doubtful; uncertain

chasm a very large gap or difference

chaste morally pure; abstaining from sex

chasten to cause to be more humble

chastise to criticize severely

chastity the condition of being morally pure; abstention from sex

chattel a personal possession

chauvinist a person who believes unreasonably in the superiority of his or her own group

checkered marked by both good and bad periods in the past

cheeky disrespectful; rude

cherubic having a round, pretty face like a child

chiaroscuro light and shade in a painting or photograph

chic fashionable; stylish

chicanery deception by trickery

chichi fashionable; showy

chide to scold

chimera a hope or dream that will never be realized

chisel to cheat or trick

chivalrous honorable and courteous toward women

chockablock very full of people or things

choleric very angry; bad-tempered

choreography the art of creating ballet or other dances

chortle to laugh in delight

chromatic pertaining to color

chromosome any of the tiny threadlike structures found in all living cells and carrying the genes that determine heredity

chronic (esp. of a disease) continuing for a long time

chronicle (n) a record of historical events

chronicle (v) to make a record, esp. of historical events

chronological arranged in the order of events as they happened

churlish rude and unpleasant

churn (of a stockbroker) to trade a customer's securities excessively

cinema a movie theater

cipher zero; a person or thing of no value

circa (in dates) approximately; about

circadian pertaining to rhythmic cycles of approximately 24 hours

circuitous not direct; roundabout

circumcision (of a male) removal of the foreskin of the penis; (of a female) removal of the clitoris or labia

circumference the distance around a circle, or the distance around the widest part of a circular object

circumlocution an indirect way of saying something

circumnavigate to sail or fly all the way around; to maneuver around something

circumscribe to severely limit

circumspect careful to consider possible consequences; cautious

circumstantial (of evidence) providing information that is not direct proof but is based on related events

circumvent to find a way to avoid

cirrhosis a serious and chronic disease of the liver

citadel a fortress or stronghold

civil not military or religious; polite and formal

cite to quote someone or something as an authority; to summon before a court of law; to praise officially

clairvoyant a person who claims to have the power to perceive things that other people cannot see

clamber to climb with difficulty, using the hands and feet

clamor a loud complaint or demand

clandestine done in secret

clannish inclined to associate with

members of one's own group

claptrap foolish, meaningless talk

claque a group of self-seeking flatterers

clarify to make clear or easier to
understand

clarion loud and clear, like the sound of a
trumpet

claustrophobia an abnormal fear of being
in small, enclosed spaces

cleave to split, as by a sudden blow; to
cling to

cleft divided; split

clemency mercy; leniency

clergy the group of people trained for
religious service

cleric a member of the clergy, as a priest

cliché an overused expression or idea

climacteric onset of the decrease in the
ability to reproduce

climactic relating to a climax

climatic relating to climate

clime climate

clinical objective and unemotional

clique a small, closed social group

clitoris a small erectile organ of the
genitals of a woman

cloak to conceal or keep secret

cloddish stupid and awkward

cloister a place of religious seclusion, as in
a monastery

closure the act of closing or ending

clout power and influence

cloven split into two parts

cloying too sweet or sentimental

coagulate to change from a liquid into a
more solid state

coalesce to grow together so as to form a
single whole

coalition a group of political factions
united for a particular purpose

cobble to put something together in a hurry

coda a concluding section or summation

coddle to overprotect

codicil a supplement to a will

codify to arrange laws or rules into a system

coerce to force someone to do something

coeval of the same age; existing at the same time

coexist to live or exist together at the same time or in the same place

cogent (of an argument) clearly expressed and convincing

cogitate to spend time thinking carefully about something

cognate related in origin, as French and Spanish

cognition the process of thinking or perceiving

cognizance knowledge or awareness

cognoscenti persons who have superior knowledge of a particular subject, esp. in the arts

cohabit to live together as if married

coherent logical and clear

cohesion a holding together; unity

cohort a group of persons who share common needs, goals or characteristics

coiffure a style of arranging the hair

coincide to happen at the same time; to be the same or similar

coincidence a chance occurrence of two events at the same time

coitus sexual intercourse

collaborate to work together for a particular purpose; to cooperate with an enemy

collage a work of art in which various materials or objects are pasted on a flat surface

collate to arrange papers in correct order

collateral (n) property promised as security for a loan

collateral (adj) accompanying; additional

collective relating to or shared by a group; forming a whole

collegial marked by a feeling of friendship and cooperation among colleagues

collegiate relating to college or college students

collegium a group of officials with equal rank

colloquial (of language) informal; conversational

colloquy a conversation or meeting

collusion a secret agreement for fraudulent purposes

coltish young, energetic, and awkward

comatose being in a state of deep unconsciousness

combatant a person who fights in a war

combative eager to fight or argue

combustion the process of burning

comely (of a woman) pleasing in appearance; attractive

comestibles articles of food

comeuppance a deserved punishment

comity mutual courtesy, as between nations

commandeer to seize possession or control of, esp. for military use

commemorate to honor the memory of a person, group, or event

commendable worthy of praise

commensurate equal to; in proportion to

commingle to blend together

commiserate to sympathize

commitment a promise or obligation; deep loyalty

commodious having a lot of space

commodity an article of trade or commerce

commonality a feature or characteristic held in common

commonplace ordinary; usual

commonweal the public good

communal belonging to or used by a group of people

communicable capable of being passed to others

communion the act of sharing thoughts or feelings

compact a formal agreement

comparable capable of being compared; similar

comparative measured in relation to something else

compatible able to exist or work together successfully

compatriot a person from one's own country

compel to force to do something; to make necessary

compendium a brief summary of a larger work; a list of a number of items

compensation payment in money or satisfaction

compensatory serving to compensate for injury or loss

competent having adequate skill or knowledge

compile to put together information from various sources

complacent contented with oneself; self-satisfied; unconcerned

complaisant inclined to please or oblige others

complement to be an appropriate addition that makes something more complete or attractive

compliant inclined to yield to the requests of others

complicity participation in wrongdoing

component one of the parts that form a whole

comportment behavior; manners

composite something that is made of

various different parts

composure calmness and control

compound to add to something; increase

comprehend to understand; to take in

comprehensive including everything necessary; complete

compress to press into a smaller space; to make shorter

comprise to include or contain

compromise (n) an agreement in which there is adjustment of opposing demands on each side

compromise (v) to put in a position of harm or difficulty; jeopardize

compulsion an irresistible urge or impulse

compulsory required

compunction a slight, uneasy sense of guilt

compute to calculate

concatenation a linking together, as in a chain

concave curved inward

concede to acknowledge that something is true; to yield or grant something to someone

conceit too much pride or self-confidence; a thought or idea

conceive to invent a plan or idea; to become pregnant

concentric having the same center

concerted planned or done together with others

concierge a member of a hotel staff who helps guests with problems or requests

conciliatory aimed at pleasing or winning back favor

concise brief and clear

conclave a private or secret meeting

conclusive ending any doubt or uncertainty

concoct to make by combining several different ingredients or parts; to invent

concomitant happening together with something else

concordance an alphabetical collection of the words used in a written work

concourse a large open space for crowds, as at a transportation facility

concrete being about actual things or situations; dealing with facts and certainties

concubine a woman who lives with a man as if married

concupiscence sexual desire; lust

concur to have the same opinion; agree

concurrent happening at the same time

condemn to criticize strongly; to sentence to a particular punishment; to declare a building unfit for use

condescend to treat others in a self-important manner; to do something that is considered beneath one's social position

condiment a substance used as a seasoning for food

condolence an expression of sympathy

condone to forgive or overlook

conducive helping to produce a specific result

conduit a channel through which anything is carried or conveyed

confabulate to talk together informally

confederate an accomplice in wrongdoing

confer to consult together; to award, as an honor

confidant someone with whom one shares personal matters or secrets

confide to tell secrets to someone

confiscate to seize something by authority

conflagration a large fire

conflate to combine two or more things into one; merge

confluence a flowing together

conformity agreement; harmony

confound to confuse or surprise; to mix up

confute to prove a person or thing to be wrong

congeal to change from a liquid to a solid; to take shape

congenial friendly and pleasant

congenital existing at birth

conglomerate a large corporation made up of many different businesses

conglomeration a large collection or mass of many different things

congregation a gathering of people, esp. for a religious service

congruent corresponding; agreeing

conjecture formation of an opinion without enough evidence; a guess

conjoined joined together

conjugal related to marriage

conjunct closely associated; conjoined

conjure to make something appear as if by magic

connive to cooperate secretly

connoisseur a person who has expert knowledge and judgment in matters of taste

connote (of a word) to suggest something in addition to the literal meaning

connubial connected with marriage

consanguinity relationship by descent from a common ancestor

conscientious careful and thorough

conscionable conforming to one's conscience

conscript to draft into the armed forces

consecrate to make holy

consecutive following one after the other in order

consensual by mutual agreement

consensus general agreement

consequence the result of an action; importance or significance

consequential important; significant

consequently as a result; therefore

conservancy an organization designated to preserve natural resources

conservation preservation of natural resources

conservative tending to preserve existing conditions, institutions, or styles

consigliere an adviser to a leader of the Mafia

consign to entrust to another's custody; to set apart

console a cabinet or panel that houses the controls for electronic or mechanical equipment

consolidate to combine into one unit; to make secure and strong

consonance accord or agreement

consort (n) a wife or husband, esp. of a ruler

consort (v) to associate with

consortium a group of companies formed to carry out an enterprise requiring large amounts of capital

conspicuous very noticeable; attracting attention

conspire to plan secretly with others to commit a wrongful act

consternation a confusing feeling of surprise or dismay

constituency a group of voters

constituent making up part of a whole

constraint something that restricts or prevents

construe to understand something in a particular way

consume to eat or drink; to use up

consummate (adj) complete in every way; highly skilled

consummate (v) to bring to completion

contagious tending to spread

contaminate to make impure or unclean; pollute

contemplate to think about something seriously; to look forward to something

contemporaneous happening or existing during the same period of time

contempt a strong feeling of dislike and lack of respect; scorn

contend to compete; to struggle against; to assert that something is true

contention an argument or controversy; a statement put forth in an argument

contentious causing or likely to cause disagreement

context the part of a text that surrounds a word or phrase and clarifies its meaning; the setting of an event

contiguous next to or touching; adjoining

continence self-restraint or abstinence; ability to control bowel and bladder functions

contingent depending on something else not yet known; possible but not certain

continuity an uninterrupted series; smooth change or development

continuum something that continues without interruption

contort to twist severely out of shape

contraband goods that are prohibited by law from being imported or exported

contraception the use of any method that prevents conception

contradict to state the opposite of what has been said; to be opposed to or inconsistent with

contraption an awkward-looking mechanical device

contrary completely different; opposed

contravene to break a law or rule

contretemps an unlucky or embarrassing occurrence or situation

contrite feeling regret for having done something bad

contrive to make or bring about cleverly

controversy a strong disagreement, esp. a public one

contumacious willfully stubborn and rebellious

contumely insolent; insulting

contusion a bruise

conundrum a riddle or puzzle

convalescence gradual recovery after an illness or injury

convene to gather together; assemble

conventional approved by general usage; following accepted practice; (of weapons) not nuclear

converge to come together in one place; to move toward the same conclusion or result

conversant familiar with

converse (n) the opposite

converse (v) to talk

conversely on the opposite side

convey to transport; to make known

conviction a strongly held belief

convivial friendly and cheerful

convoke to call together

convoluted having many turns or twists; complicated; intricate

convulsion an uncontrolled fit; a violent upheaval

co-opt to appropriate as one's own

copacetic very satisfactory; fine

copious in large amounts

cop-out avoidance of a responsibility or commitment

copulate to have sex

coquette a female flirt

cordial polite and gracious; an alcoholic drink

cordon a line of police officers, soldiers, etc., placed around an area to enclose it

cornucopia an abundant supply

corollary an expected outcome or effect

corporeal of the body; physical

corpulent fat

corpus a complete collection of writings

correlation a connection or relation between two or more things

correspond to be very similar or equivalent

corroborate to confirm with additional evidence

corrosive harmful or destructive

corrugated bent into folds or ridges

cortege a ceremonial procession

coruscate to flash brightly; sparkle

cosmic relating to the universe or outer space; vast

cosmopolitan (of a city) made up of people or elements from many parts of the world; (of a person) having wide experience; sophisticated

cosset to pamper; coddle

coterie an exclusive group of people; clique

countenance (n) the expression of the face

countenance (v) to give approval to; condone

counteract to lessen the effect of something by means of an opposing action

counterfeit fake; false

countermand to revoke a command by giving a contrary order

counterpart a person or thing that corresponds to another in function or position

counterpoint any element that is contrasted with another

countervail to act against with equal force

coup an unexpected, highly successful achievement

coup de grâce (koo duh GRAHS) a death blow; a final or decisive stroke

coupe a small two-door car

couple to join or combine

courier any means of carrying messages, news, etc., regularly

courtesan paramour of noble, aristocratic, or wealthy men

couturier a person who designs and sells fashionable clothes for women

coven a group of witches

covenant a formal agreement

covert secret; hidden

covetous strongly desiring something that belongs to another

cower to crouch or draw back in fear

coy pretending to be shy or modest

cozen to trick or deceive

crabbed difficult to read or understand

crapulous grossly excessive in eating or drinking

crass stupid and insensitive; outrageously obvious

craven extremely cowardly

credence acceptance as true; belief

credentials verbal or written evidence of rights, status, or authority

credible able to be believed or trusted

creditable deserving of respect

credence belief

credo a system of belief

credulity willingness to believe or trust

credulous easily deceived; gullible

creed a set of beliefs

crepuscular pertaining to or resembling twilight

crescendo a gradual increase in loudness

crestfallen disappointed and discouraged

cretin a very stupid person

crevice a narrow crack or opening

crib to copy answers or information from someone else's work

cri de coeur (cree duh coor) an anguished cry of distress

cringe to draw back in fear

criterion (pl. **criteria**) a rule or standard used to judge something

critique a critical review or evaluation

crone an ugly old woman

crotchety bad-tempered; irritable

croupier a person who works at a gambling table in a casino

crucial extremely important

cruciform shaped like a cross

crux the central or most important point

cryptic having a hidden meaning; mysterious

cubicle a very small compartment of a larger room

cuckold a man whose wife is unfaithful

cudgel a short, thick club or stick

cuisine a style of cooking

cul-de-sac a narrow street that is closed at one end

culinary related to the kitchen and cooking

cull to select or choose; to remove unwanted things from

culmination the highest point or degree

culpable worthy of blame; guilty

culprit someone who is guilty of an offense

cumbersome bulky and difficult to handle

cum combined with

cum laude with academic honors

cumulative increasing by one addition after another

cunnilingus oral stimulation of the female genitals

cupidity greed

curator a person in charge of a museum, library, or zoo

curmudgeon a bad-tempered old person

curriculum the courses of study offered at a college

curry favor to seek to gain some advantage by flattery

cursive   written with letters that are joined
   together

cursory   hasty and superficial

curt   rudely brief

curtail   to reduce or limit

cynic   a person who believes that people are
   motivated only by selfishness

cynosure   one who strongly attracts
   attention or admiration

=D=

dabble   to engage in an activity casually or briefly

daft   ridiculous; crazy

dais   a raised platform

dalliance   a brief, casual romantic relationship

dally   to toy with an idea; to waste time

dank   unpleasantly damp and cold

dapper   (of a man) neatly dressed

dashing   stylish and energetic

dastardly   cowardly and mean

data   information, esp. facts and figures stored and processed by a computer

daub   to spread a soft, sticky substance on something

daunting   discouraging; scary

dauntless   not easily discouraged; fearless

deadlock   a situation in which agreement cannot be reached between opposing parties in a negotiation

dearth   a lack or scarcity

debacle   a complete failure

debase   to reduce in quality or value

debauch   to corrupt another's chastity or virtue; seduce

debilitate   to make weak

debonair   gracious and charming

debride   (di.BREED)   to remove dead tissue from a wound

debrief   to question in detail in order to obtain information about a mission

debunk   to show that something is false

debutante   a young woman who is formally presented into society

decadent   having low moral standards

decapitate   to cut off the head

decease   death

deciduous   shedding leaves at the end of

the growing season

decimate to destroy a large part of a population

decipher to discover the meaning of

decisive conclusive; unmistakable

declaim to express forcefully

déclassé of a lower class or status

declivity a downward slope

decoction an extract obtained by boiling

decolletage the low neckline of a dress

decompose to decay

deconstruct to break down into constituent parts; to analyze

decor the style of a room or house

decorous showing proper behavior

decorum calm and proper behavior

decoy a person or thing used to mislead or deceive

decree an official order

decrepit broken-down; worn-out

decry to criticize or condemn

deduce to reach an answer by reasoning

deduct to take away a part from a total

deem to consider or judge

deface to damage the surface or appearance of something

de facto existing in fact; true or real

defame to damage someone's reputation with lies

default (n) a setting used by a computer unless a different setting is chosen

default (v) to fail to do something, such as pay an obligation on time

defeatism an attitude of feeling unable to succeed in life

defecate to empty the bowels

defect (n) a flaw, problem, or lack

defect (v) to abandon a country or group, esp. for political reasons

defendant a person who is accused of wrongdoing and is taken to court

defenestration the act of throwing

someone out of a window

defer to postpone

deference respect and politeness

deficient lacking

deficit the amount by which money spent is more than money received

defile to spoil the beauty or purity of something

definitive clear and conclusive; complete

deflect to cause to change direction

defoliant a chemical that causes plants to lose their leaves

defraud to take something by illegal means; swindle

defray to pay the cost of something

deft skillful and quick

defunct no longer functioning or living

defuse to make less dangerous or tense

defy to oppose or resist openly

degenerate a corrupt, immoral person

degrade to lower in quality or dignity

dehydrate to lose water or moisture

deify to make into a god

deign to do something that is considered beneath one's dignity

deism belief in the existence of a God

deity a god or goddess

déjà vu the feeling that you have already experienced something that is happening for the first time

dejected in low spirits; sad

de jure having legal existence

delectable delicious; delightful

delectation great pleasure and enjoyment

delegate (n) a representative, as of a government or political party

delegate (v) to entrust something to another person

delete to erase or eliminate

deleterious harmful

deliberation serious discussion

delineate to describe in detail

delinquency law-breaking behavior, esp. by young people

delirium a state of confusion resulting from high fever; a state of great excitement

delude to deceive

delusion a false belief

delve to search deeply; examine

demagogue a political leader who wins power by exciting people's prejudices and fears

demarcate to show the limits of

démarche a formal appeal or protest

demean to lower in dignity or social standing; humiliate

demeanor way of behaving; manner

demented mentally ill

demigod a being that is part human and part god

demimonde unethical persons of low status, esp. prostitutes

demise death

demitasse strong black coffee served in a small cup

democracy a system of government in which power is held by the people or their elected representatives

demography the study of the characteristics of human populations, such as average age, income, and birth rates

demolish to destroy

demonize to make a person or group seem to be completely evil

demonstrable able to be proved

demoralize to weaken the confidence of

demotic (of a language) in a form used by ordinary people

demur to express disagreement or refusal

demure modest and well-behaved

denature to deprive something of its natural qualities

denigrate to speak against the reputation or quality of someone or something

denizen a person or animal that lives in a particular place

denote to show clearly; indicate

denouement the final outcome or result

denounce to criticize strongly and openly

denude to make bare, as land

depict to describe or show

depilatory a liquid or cream that removes hair from the body

deplete to empty out; use up

deplore to express strong disapproval of; to express sorrow or regret over

deploy to put in a position of readiness, esp. for military action

deport to expel from a country

deportment personal conduct; behavior

depose to remove from power

deposition a formal written statement for use in a court of law

depraved morally corrupt; evil

deprecate to express disapproval of; belittle

depreciate to lose value over time

depredation plunder and destruction

deputation a group of people sent to speak for others

deracinate to uproot or displace

deranged mentally unstable; insane

derelict a homeless person; an abandoned property

dereliction failure to do what one should

deride to make fun of; mock

de rigueur strictly required by fashion or custom

derision contemptuous laughter; ridicule

derivative lacking originality

derive to obtain or come from something else

derogatory expressing a low opinion; critical

dervish a member of a Muslim religious order that engages in whirling dances

descant to comment at great length

descry to discover or detect

desecrate to damage something sacred

desiccated thoroughly dried or dried up

desideratum something wanted or needed

designate to indicate or point out; to appoint

desist to stop doing something

desolate (of a place) barren or deserted; (of a person) lonely and sad

despicable deserving contempt; hateful

despise to regard with contempt and loathing

despite in spite of; not prevented by

despoil to strip of possessions or value; plunder

despondent feeling depressed and hopeless

despot a cruel ruler; tyrant

destiny the predetermined course or end result of one's life

destitute lacking food, clothing, and shelter

desultory lacking consistency or purpose; disconnected

détente a period of relaxed tensions between hostile nations

deter to prevent or discourage from doing something

deteriorate to become worse

determination firmness of purpose; a finding or conclusion

determine to control or influence; to conclude or decide

deterrent something that prevents or discourages

detest to hate

detonate to explode

detract to take away from the importance or quality of

detriment harm or damage

detritus waste material; debris

deus ex machina something unlikely that provides a sudden solution to any problem

devastate to destroy; to overwhelm

deviant a person whose sexual behavior differs from socially accepted standards

deviate to vary from the rule or standard; stray

devious not direct or honest; shifty

devise to figure out a plan

devoid lacking; empty

devolve to transfer a duty or responsibility to another

devotee a fan or admirer

devout deeply religious; sincere

dexterity skill or ability in using the hands or the mind

diabolical extremely clever or wicked

dialectic a method of argument for discovering the truth

diaphanous (of cloth) delicate and sheer

Diaspora a group's flight or migration from a country or region, esp. the Jews exodus from Babylon

diatribe a severely critical verbal attack

dichotomy a division into two opposing parts

dictation the act of speaking something aloud for another person to write down

dictum an authoritative command; a short saying

didactic intended to teach; moralizing too much

differentiate to describe or discern differences

diffident shy and lacking self-confidence

diffuse widely spread out

dignitary a person of high rank or position

digress to turn away from the main subject in speaking or writing

dilapidated   fallen into decay through age and neglect

dilate   to make larger; widen

dilatory   slow and tending to cause delay

dilettante   a person who takes up an activity or subject in a casual manner

diligent   showing dedicated and persistent effort

dilute   to weaken by adding something, such as water; to reduce in intensity, purity, or value

diminutive   very small

din   loud and confusing noise

dint   force; power

diocese   the area or group of churches under the control of a bishop

Dionysian   wildly uninhibited; frenzied

diplomacy   the management of relationships between countries; skill in dealing with people in a tactful way

dipsomaniac   an alcoholic

dire   extremely serious

dirge   a slow, sad piece of music

disabuse   to correct someone's wrong idea

disaffected   no longer content or loyal

disarming   winning favor or trust; charming

disarray   a state of disorder or confusion

disavow   to deny knowledge of or connection with

disburse   to pay out money, as from a fund

discern   to see or understand something that is not clear

discerning   able to make good judgments; perceptive

disciple   a person who accepts and spreads the teachings of a leader

disclaim   to deny connection with or responsibility for; to give up a legal right

disclose   to make known

discomfit   to distress or confuse

disconcert   to disturb the confidence and

calm of

disconsolate very sad; hopeless

discord lack of agreement; an unpleasant mixing of sounds or notes

discourse conversation; discussion

discredit to refuse to accept as accurate; to cause a loss of belief in the authority of; to hurt the reputation of

discreet showing caution and good judgment in what one says and does

discrepancy a lack of agreement between two things that should be the same

discrete separate; distinct

discretion good judgment

discriminate to see the differences between; to show prejudice against

discriminating showing careful judgment or good taste

discursive moving from topic to topic

disdain the feeling that someone or something deserves no respect or attention

disembark to get off a ship or airplane

disenfranchise to take away someone's rights, esp. the right to vote

disengage to cause to become separate; to cease being connected

disentangle to free from tangles or confusion

disfigure to spoil the appearance of, esp. the face

disgorge to pour out forcefully

disgruntled discontented and disappointed

dishabille (dis.a.BEEL) the state of being partially or carelessly dressed

dishearten to discourage

disheveled (of one's appearance) untidy; messy

disillusion to take away someone's faith and trust

disinclined unwilling sincerity; insincere

disjointed   (of words or ideas) not well connected

dislodge   to remove from a position, esp. by force

dislocate   to force out of its normal place or condition, as a bone

dismal   causing gloom or depression; very bad

dismay   to make downhearted or greatly troubled

dismember   to cut or tear off the parts of a body; to divide into pieces

dismissive   showing indifference or disregard

disorient   to cause to lose one's bearings; confuse

disparage   to speak of as having little value or importance

disparate   completely different; unconnected

disparity   lack of similarity; difference or inequality

dispassionate   not affected by emotional involvement

dispel   to cause to disappear, as fears or doubts

dispensable   not essential or necessary

dispensation   release from an obligation or rule

disperse   to scatter in various directions; to disappear

dispirited   depressed; discouraged

disport   to amuse oneself in a playful way; frolic

disposed   inclined or willing

disposition   the usual mood or attitude of a person; final settlement of a matter

disproportionate   too large or small compared to something else

disputatious   argumentative

dispute   to debate or argue about something; to question the validity of

disquiet to make uneasy or anxious

disquisition a long and detailed explanation

disrepair the condition of needing repair

disreputable having a bad reputation; not to be trusted

disrepute loss of reputation; disgrace

dissect to cut apart for examination; to analyze or criticize in detail

dissemble to hide one's true feelings or motives

disseminate to make known widely

dissension difference of opinion; disagreement

dissent disagreement; opposition

dissertation a long, formal piece of writing on a particular subject

dissident a person who publicly disagrees, as with a government

dissimulate to conceal under a false appearance

dissipate to scatter in various directions; to spend or use wastefully

dissipated characterized by excessive self-indulgence

dissociate to consider as separate and not connected

dissolute indulging in immoral conduct

dissonance an unpleasant combination of sounds; lack of agreement

dissuade to persuade not to do something

distaff pertaining to women or the female line of descent

distend to swell by internal pressure

distinct clearly separate and different

distinction a clear difference; excellence or honor

distinctive serving to set apart; different and unusual

distinguished recognized as being excellent; dignified in manner

distort to change from the usual or

intended shape or meaning

distract to draw the attention away

distracted very upset or troubled

distraught extremely anxious or upset

dither a state of nervous excitement and confusion

diurnal occurring each day; active during the day

diva a female opera star

diverge to separate and go in different directions

divers various or several

diverse different from each other; varied

diversity variety

divert to cause to change direction; to amuse or entertain

divertissement an entertainment

divest to free oneself of assets or investments; to take away rights or property

divination the art of foretelling the future by supernatural means

divisive tending to cause disagreement and division

divulge to make known something that was secret

docent a trained guide who conducts visitors through a museum

docile easy to train or control

docket a list of cases to be dealt with in a court

doctrinaire holding to doctrines or theories without regard for practical matters

doctrine a principle or set of beliefs held by a religious or political group; a statement of government policy

doddering shaky and unsteady, esp. from old age

doff to take off

dogged very determined

doggerel worthless poetry

dogma an established belief or principle that must be accepted without question

dogmatic insisting on one's own beliefs as the only truth; opinionated

doldrums a condition of depressed inactivity

doleful very sad

dolorous seeming sad or causing sorrow; mournful

dolt a stupid person

domain an area of control, interest, or activity

domicile one's home

dominion the right to rule or control

doppelganger a ghostly double of a living person

dormant in an inactive state

dossier a collection of papers containing detailed information on a person or subject

dotage a time of mental decline associated with old age

dote to show too much affection

double entendre a word or expression that can be understood in two ways

doughty brave and determined

dour unsmiling; sullen

douse plunged into or covered with a liquid

dovetail to fit together closely

dowager a dignified elderly woman, esp. a widow with property

dowdy shabby and old-fashioned

download to transfer data from one computer to another

dowry money or property brought to a marriage by a woman

doyenne a woman who is the senior member of a group or profession

draconian (of laws, punishment, etc.) unusually severe; cruel

dragoon to force to do something

dramatis personae the cast of characters in a play

dramaturgy the art of dramatic composition

drawn looking very tired or ill; haggard

dread to feel fear or extreme anxiety about something in the future

dreadnought a type of battleship; something very large and powerful

dregs the sediment at the bottom of a liquid; the part of something that is undesirable or worthless

drivel stupid talk; nonsense

droll amusing in an odd way

drone a person who lives on the labor of others; to talk in a boring way

dross something useless or worthless

drought a long dry period

drudgery hard, menial work

dubious feeling or causing doubt or uncertainty

ducat a ticket

ductile (of metals) easily bent or molded; easily persuaded or influenced

duenna a governess or chaperone

dulcet (of tones) soft and musical

dullard a stupid person

dun to keep asking someone for repayment of a debt

dupe (n) someone who has been tricked

dupe (v) to trick or deceive

duplicity deliberate deceptiveness, esp. in saying different things to two people

duress force or threats

dwell to speak or think about something at length

dwindle to become less or smaller

dybbuk a wandering soul believed to enter and control a living person

dynamic forceful; very active or intense

dynasty a family that remains powerful in politics or business through successive generations

dysfunction   abnormal or imperfect
functioning of a system, social unit, or part
of the body

dyslexia   a learning disorder that impairs
the ability to read

dyspepsia   indigestion

dystopia   an imaginary place where people
lead brutish lives

=E=

earmark to set aside for a particular purpose

earshot the normal distance within which a sound or the voice can be heard

easement a right held by a property owner to make limited use of a portion of another's land

ebullient lively and happy

ecce homo behold the man

eccentric odd or unusual

ecclesiastical related to church matters

echelon a level of authority within an organization

eclectic choosing the best from various sources

eclipse to overshadow in importance

ecology the study of the relationship between living things and their environment

ecru very light brown; beige

ecstatic extremely happy

ectomorph a thin person

ectoplasm a substance that is said to produce and surround ghosts

ecumenical worldwide in extent or influence; tending to promote Christian unity

edict proclamation or command from an authority

edifice a large, impressive building; a long-established system

edify to instruct or enlighten

educe to draw forth or bring out; develop

effable able to be uttered or expressed

efface to wipe out or do away with; obliterate

effectual producing the desired effect

effectuate to bring about; effect

effeminate (of a man) having qualities or tastes considered to be feminine

effervescent high-spirited; lively

effete weak and decadent

efficacious effective; practical

effigy a crude figure of a hated person

effleurage a type of light, brushing massage

efflorescence a period of flowering or high development

effluent liquid waste

effluvium an unpleasant vapor or odor

effrontery shameless rudeness

effulgent shining forth brightly; radiant

effusive excessive in expressing feelings

egalitarian one who believes in equal rights and opportunity for all

egocentric concerned only with oneself; self-centered

egoism excessive concern for one's own interests

egotism an exaggerated sense of one's importance

egotist a conceited, boastful person

egregious extremely bad; outrageous

egress an exit

eidetic marked by vivid recall of visual images

ejaculate to speak out suddenly; to discharge sperm

eke to manage to make enough for one's needs

elaborate to provide more information or detail

élan liveliness and style

elapse (of time) to go by

elation extreme happiness and excitement

electorate all the persons qualified to vote in an election

elegiac mournful

elegy a poem or song expressing sorrow for the dead

elemental basic or fundamental

elephantine very large

elfin small and delicate

elicit to bring out; evoke

elide to omit an unstressed vowel; to delete a written word

eliminate to remove or take away

elite those in the highest levels of a society

elixir a magical substance believed to cure all ills

ellipse an oval

elocution the art of public speaking and careful pronunciation

elongate to make or become longer; lengthen

elope to run off to get married

eloquence persuasive and fluent speech

elucidate to explain and make clear

elude to avoid or escape from; to be difficult to find or remember

elusive hard to express or describe

elysian blissful; delightful

emaciated very thin and weak, esp. from lack of food

emanate to come from

emancipate to free from slavery or oppression; liberate

emasculate to castrate; to deprive of strength and vigor

embalm to treat a dead body with preservatives; to keep something unchanged

embargo a temporary ban on trade with another nation or on giving information

embark to go aboard a ship or plane; to begin a journey or new activity

embattled in a fight with one's enemies or critics

embed to fix firmly into a substance

embellish to make more beautiful or interesting by adding details; to add imaginative details to a story or statement

embezzle   to steal money that has been entrusted to one's care

emblazon   to decorate something with bold markings

emblematic   serving as a symbol; symbolic

embody   to symbolize or personify; to include as part of a system or whole

embroider   to add imaginative details to; exaggerate

embroil   to involve someone in an argument or difficulty

embryo   the earliest stage of development of a fertilized egg in the uterus

embryonic   in an early undeveloped stage

emend   to correct or improve written text

emeritus   retired but keeping an honorary title

emetic   a substance that causes vomiting

emigrate   to leave one's country to settle in another

emigré   a person who has fled his or her country for political reasons

eminence   a position of great distinction or superiority

éminence grise   someone who has secret power or influence

eminent   widely recognized as being of high rank or achievement; distinguished

eminent domain   the right of the state to take and pay for private property for public use

emissary   a person sent on a mission as a representative of a country or another person

emission   something sent out, as into the air; a discharge

emollient   a substance that soothes and softens the skin

emote   to portray or pretend emotion

empathy   the ability to share another's feelings

emphasis special importance or stress placed on something

empirical based on what is seen or experienced rather than on theory

empower to give legal or official authority to

emulate to try to equal or excel, esp. by imitation

enamored filled with love

encapsulate to express in a brief summary

enclave a small, distinct area that is enclosed within a larger area

encomium an expression of high praise

encompass to encircle or surround; to include

encounter to come upon unexpectedly; to come up against, as a difficulty

encroach to go beyond former limits

encumber to burden so as to make action or performance difficult

endeavor a serious effort or attempt

endemic common within a particular area or group, as a disease

endogenous developing from conditions within

endomorph a person of large size

endorse to give approval of; support

endure to continue despite hardship; to survive for a long time; to put up with

enervate to drain of energy; weaken

enfeeble to make feeble; weaken

enfranchise to provide with the right to vote

engender to bring into being; produce

engorge to overfill, esp. with blood

engrossing occupying one's attention completely

engulf to surround and cover completely; overwhelm

enhance to improve or make greater, as in appearance or value

enigma something that is hard to

understand or explain; a mystery or puzzle

enjoin   to prescribe a course of action with authority; to prohibit or prevent

enlighten   to provide with intellectual or spiritual understanding

en masse   all together in a group

enmesh   to entangle or catch as in a net

enmity   hatred

ennoble   to elevate in rank, character, or dignity

ennui   a feeling of weariness and boredom

enormity   very great size or importance

enormous   extremely large

enrage   to make very angry; infuriate

enrapture   to fill with delight

enrich   to improve in quality by adding something desirable, as nutrients

en route   on the way

ensconce   to place oneself firmly in a particular place

ensemble   a group of musicians, dancers, or actors who perform together; a matching outfit or costume

enslave   to make a slave of; to control completely

ensnare   to catch as in a trap

ensue   to follow as a consequence or result

entail   to make necessary; require

entangle   to involve in a difficult situation

entente   a friendly agreement

enthrall   to hold the interest or attention completely; captivate

entice   to attract or persuade by arousing hope or desire; lure

entitle   to allow or authorize; to give a name or title to

entity   something that has its own independent existence

entomb   to bury

entourage   (on.too.RAZH)   a group of people who accompany and assist an important person

entrap   to attract into difficulty or harm

entreaty   a serious and sincere request; a plea

entree   the main course of a meal; special permission to enter a place

entrench   to establish firmly or securely

entre nous   (on.truh NOO)   between ourselves; confidentially

entrepreneur   a person who starts, manages, and assumes the risks of a business

entropy   a state of disorder or disorganization in a system

entwine   to wrap around

enumerate   to count off one by one; list

enunciate   to pronounce clearly; to state precisely

envelop   to cover or surround completely

envious   wanting to have what another person has

environs   the surrounding area, esp. of a city

envision or **envisage**   to picture in the mind

envoy   a diplomatic representative of a government

eon   an extremely long period of time

ephemeral   lasting only a brief time

epic (n)   a long poem, book, or film about heroic adventures

epic (adj)   extremely large; tremendous

epidemic   spreading rapidly and widely

epicene   belonging to or having the characteristics of both sexes

epicenter   the exact center of a major event, as of an earthquake

epicure   a person who has a refined taste in food and wine

epidermis   the thin outer layer of the skin

epigram   a short poem or saying that expresses a clever idea

epigraph a saying or quotation put at the beginning of a work to suggest its theme

epilogue a short section added to the end of a work, usually telling what happens after the main story ends

epiphany sudden insight into the reality of something

episode one in a series of events

episodic divided into separate parts or sections

epistemology the study of the nature and limits of knowledge

epistle a letter

epitaph an inscription on a gravestone

epithet a term used to describe a person or thing, often negatively

epitome (e.PIT.uh.me) the typical example of a quality, class, or type

e pluribus unum one out of many

epoch a long period in history marked by important events and great changes

eponymous (of characters in books and plays) having the same name as the title

equable even-tempered; calm

equanimity calmness; composure

equate to make or consider the same or equivalent

equestrian a person who rides horses

equilateral having sides of the same length

equilibrium a state of balance or stability

equinox either of the two times in the year when day and night are of equal length

equip to supply with what is needed

equipoise equal distribution of weight; balance

equitable fair and reasonable to all concerned

equity fairness or justice; the value of a business or property less the money owed against it

equivalent equal in amount, value, or

meaning

equivocal able to be interpreted in different ways; ambiguous

equivocate to use language that is intentionally unclear or misleading

eradicate to get rid of; destroy

ergo therefore

ergonomics an applied science concerned with the design of environments, tools, and machines to enable people to work efficiently, safely and comfortably

erode to wear away; to weaken or lessen

erogenous arousing sexual desire

Eros the Greek god of sexual love

erotic related to sexual desire

errant wandering off course

errata errors in printed matter

erratic inconsistent or irregular

erroneous incorrect; mistaken

ersatz serving as a substitute; artificial

erstwhile previous

erudite having great knowledge; scholarly

erupt to burst forth violently

escalate to increase or cause to increase in scope or intensity

escapade a carefree or risky adventure

escarpment a steep slope or cliff

eschatology the branch of theology concerned with the end of the world

eschew to avoid; shun

esoteric intended for or understood by only a small number of people

espionage the act of spying or the use of spies

esplanade a wide, level walkway, esp. along a shore

espouse to take up and support, as a cause

esprit de corps (e.spree duh KORE) the sense of pride and loyalty shared by members of a group

espy to see at a distance

essay a short written work presenting a

personal view on a particular subject

esteem to regard with respect

esthete or **aesthete** a person who fully appreciates and enjoys beauty, esp. in art

esthetic or **aesthetic** relating to the enjoyment of beauty

estimable deserving respect or admiration

estranged (of a married couple) separated

estrogen a hormone that causes the development of female characteristics and regulates the reproductive cycle

estuary the place where a river meets the sea

et al and elsewhere

et cetera and other similar things

ethereal light and delicate; heavenly

ethical morally right

ethics a set of moral principles or values

ethnic relating to a group of people that have the same racial, national, or cultural background

ethnocentrism belief in the superiority of one's own culture or ethnic group

ethos the basic character of a culture

etiolated (of plants) pale and weak

etiquette the set of rules of proper behavior in society

eugenics the study of methods of improving a breed or species, as by encouraging reproduction by individuals with desirable hereditary characteristics

eulogize to praise highly

eulogy a speech or piece of writing containing great praise, esp. for a person who has recently died

eunuch a castrated man

euphemism a word or phrase used in place of another that is considered unpleasant or offensive

euphonious pleasant-sounding

euphoria a strong feeling of happiness and well-being

eureka I've found it!

euthanasia mercy killing

evanescent lasting for only a brief time

evasive intended to deceive or elude; intentionally misleading

evenhanded dealing fairly with everyone

evident easily seen or understood

evince to show clearly; make obvious

eviscerate to remove the insides of; gut

evoke to call forth, as a feeling or memory

exacerbate to make worse or more severe

exalted having high rank or status; elevated

exasperate to anger and frustrate; irritate greatly

ex cathedra with complete authority

excavate to expose or uncover by digging

excelsior wood shavings used for packing fragile items; (Latin) ever upward

excise to remove, esp. by cutting

exclamation something said suddenly or forcefully

excommunicate to cut off from church membership by official authority

excoriate to denounce or criticize severely

excrement solid waste matter from the body

excrete to pass waste matter

excruciating intensely painful

exculpate to remove blame from

execrable very bad

execrate to detest completely

exegesis an explanation or interpretation of a text, esp. from the Bible

exemplar a typical example; a model to be imitated

exemplary worthy of imitation; outstanding

exemplify to be or give an example of something; illustrate

exfoliate to remove dead skin

exhaustive complete; thorough

exhilarate to fill with energy and excitement

exhort to urge strongly

exhume to remove a body from its burial place

exigency an urgent need

exigent requiring immediate action; urgent

exiguous scanty; meager

existentialism a system of belief that centers on the plight of the individual in a meaningless universe

exodus a departure of a large group of people

ex officio by virtue of official position

exogenous originating from outside

exonerate to free from blame

exorbitant much too high or large; excessive

exorcise to free from evil spirits

exoteric suitable for general communication; not limited to a select group

exotic foreign and unusual

expanse a very large area

expansive broad in size or scope; friendly and generous

ex parte from only one side of a dispute

expatiate to speak or write about something in great detail

expatriate a person who gives up his or her country to live in another

expectorate to spit

expedient suited to a particular purpose; based only on one's own interests

expedite to cause to be done more quickly

expend to use or spend

expendable likely to be given up; not needed

experiential derived from experience

expertise expert skill or knowledge

expiate to atone or make amends for

expletive a swear word

explicate to explain in detail

explicit clear and exact; giving all details openly

exploit (n) a brave or adventurous act

exploit (v) to use for advantage

exponent a person who represents or supports something, as a belief

exponential large and growing rapidly

expository serving to set forth or explain; explanatory

ex post facto after the fact

expostulate to express disagreement or complaint

expound to explain in detail

expropriate to take from another and use as one's own

expunge to erase or remove, as information

expurgate to remove words or passages considered offensive

exquisite very beautiful and delicate; (of pleasure or pain) intense

exsanguinate to drain of blood

extant still in existence

extemporaneous done or said without advance preparation

extensive covering a large area

extenuating lessening the severity of wrongdoing by providing a reason

extinct no longer in existence

extinguish to put out, as a fire; to destroy, as hopes

extirpate to remove or destroy completely

extol to praise highly

extortion illegal use of force or official power to obtain money or property

extract to obtain or draw out

extracurricular outside the regular program of courses

extradite (in law) to require someone to return to another state or country for trial

extramarital outside of marriage

extraneous not directly connected; irrelevant

extrapolate to guess an unknown meaning or result by using known information

extravagant spending much more than necessary; unreasonable or excessive

extremity the outermost or farthest point; (pl.) the hands and feet

extricate to free from a difficult situation

extrinsic outside of; external

extrovert a person who is sociable and outgoing

extrude to force or press outward

exuberant enthusiastic and joyful

exude to send out from inside oneself; to display, as confidence

exult to express triumphant joy; rejoice

=F=

fabricate to lie; falsify; to make, construct or assemble something

façade the front of a large building; a false appearance

facet one of the small flat surfaces cut on a gem; one of the parts or aspects of something

facetious not meant to be taken seriously; unsuitably humorous

facile done easily or too easily

facilitate to make easier or possible

facsimile an exact copy or reproduction

faction an opposing group within a larger group

factious inclined to oppose or dispute

factitious false or artificial

factoid a small, insignificant fact

factor a fact or situation that helps cause a certain result

factotum a person having many varied responsibilities

faculty the teaching staff of a college; a natural ability, esp. of the mind

fait accompli an action that has been completed and cannot be changed

fallacious not correct or true; false

fallacy a false idea or mistaken belief

fallible capable of making mistakes

fallow unproductive; dormant

falsetto an artificially high singing voice in a man

Falstaffian a bawdy, brazen, good-natured rascal

falter to lose strength or purpose; hesitate

familial relating to the whole family

famine a serious, widespread lack of food

famished extremely hungry

fanatic a person with an extreme and

uncritical enthusiasm for something

fancied   unreal; imaginary

fancier   a person with a special interest in something

fanciful   imaginative; whimsical

fanfare   a showy display

farce   a ridiculous or meaningless situation

farcical   laughable; foolish

farrago   a confused mixture

farthing   an old British coin of little value

fascism   a political system based on a dictatorship, rigid state control, and suppression of all opposition

fatal   causing death; disastrous

fastidious   paying close attention to small details; difficult to please; fussy

fatalism   the belief that all events are determined in advance and cannot be changed

fathom   to comprehend the meaning of

fatuous   foolish; stupid

fatigue   extreme tiredness or weakness

fauna   all the animals of a particular region

faux   false; artificial

faux pas   (foh pah)   a social error

fawn   to seek favor through flattery

faze   to upset or disturb

fealty   faithfulness; loyalty

feasible   possible; workable

febrile   feverish; hectic

feces   solid waste excreted from the bowels

feckless   weak or ineffective; worthless or irresponsible

fecund   fertile

feeble   lacking strength or power

feign   to pretend; to fake

feint   a movement meant to distract or deceive an opponent

feisty   energetic and spirited; tending to argue

felicitous   well-suited; apt

felicity happiness; a pleasing or skillful quality

fell to cut down

fellatio oral stimulation of the penis

felon a person guilty of a major crime

feminism belief in equal rights and opportunities for women

femme fatale (fom fahtal) a woman who is dangerously attractive to men

feng shui (fung shway) the Chinese art of determining the most harmonious sites for environments such as the home or office, and the arrangement of the furnishings they contain

feral (of animals) existing in a wild state

ferment unrest; agitation

ferocious fierce; savage

ferret to uncover by searching

fervent or **fervid** intense; passionate

fervor strong emotion or belief

fester (of a wound) to become infected; (of bad feelings) to become worse

festoon to decorate with strings or chains of flowers, ribbons, etc.

fete a large party, often held outdoors

fetid having a stale, offensive odor

fetish an object of excessive, often sexual, attention

fetter to restrict the freedom of

fettle state or condition

fetus the developed embryo in mammals

fey whimsical; strange; enchanted

fiasco a complete failure

fiat an order issued by a person in authority

fictitious false; imaginary

fiduciary a person who controls property or money for another

figment something invented or imagined

figurative not literal; metaphorical or emblematic

figurehead a person in a position of

leadership who has no real power

filch to steal something of little value

filet or **fillet** a boneless piece of fish or meat

filial of a son or daughter

filibuster a delaying tactic by a lawmaker to prevent the passage of a bill by speaking at great length

filigree delicate and detailed ornamentation of gold or silver

fillip something that causes a sudden improvement; stimulus

fin a five-dollar bill

finagle to get something through trickery or deception

finale the concluding part, as of a musical performance

fin de siècle the end of the century

finesse tact and skill; smoothness

finite limited in number or amount

firebrand a person who causes political or social unrest

firmament the sky; the heavens

fiscal relating to public money

fissiparous tending to split into factions

fissure a split or crack, as in rock

fitful irregular; disturbed

fixation an unnaturally strong preoccupation with something; obsession

flabbergast to cause to be extremely surprised or shocked

flaccid lacking firmness; weak

flack a publicist or press agent; unwelcome criticism

flagellate to whip

flag to lose energy or strength; become weak

flagrant openly bad or offensive; blatant

flagrante delicto in the act of committing the offense

flail to move the arms or legs in an uncontrolled way

flamboyant showy; bold

flatulence an accumulation of gas in the digestive tract expelled through the anus

flaunt to display with too much pride

flay to remove the skin from; to criticize severely

fledgling inexperienced; a young bird that is ready to fly

fleece to swindle or cheat

fleeting brief or quick

flighty unpredictable or impulsive in behavior

flimflam to deceive or swindle

flinty unyielding; stony

flippant carelessly disrespectful; lacking the proper seriousness

flora plants of a given area

florid very detailed or flowery; (of the complexion) too red

flotilla a large group of ships

flotsam the floating remains of a sunken ship; something unwanted or worthless

flounce to move in an exaggerated or bouncy manner

flounder to struggle clumsily or helplessly

flout to show a lack of respect for; defy

fluctuate to vary irregularly

fluent able to speak or write a language casily

fluke something good that has happened by chance

flummery complete nonsense

flummox to confuse or baffle

flush to rinse away; to become red in the face; to force a man or animal out of hiding

flux continual change

fob to palm off something inferior on someone

fogy or **fogey** a very old-fashioned or conservative person

foible a small personal fault or foolish

habit

foil (n) a person or thing that makes another's qualities more noticeable by contrast

foil (v) to prevent from being successful

foist to pass off as genuine or worthwhile

folly a foolish act or idea

foment to stir up; provoke

font a source or origin; a style of print

foolhardy foolishly bold; reckless

fop a vain, foolish man who is too interested in his appearance

forage to search for food or supplies

foray a first try at something different

forbearance patience and tolerance in a difficult situation

force majeure an overwhelming force or uncontrollable event

foreboding a sense that something bad is about to happen

foreclose (of a bank) to take possession of a property for nonpayment of a mortgage; to prevent something from being considered

forefront the most advanced or important position

forego to go before; to precede

foregoing mentioned just before; previous

foregone (of a conclusion) seen as certain or inevitable

foremost most important or leading

forensic relating to scientific methods used to discover the facts in a crime

foreplay sexual activity before intercourse

forerunner an early model of what will appear later; a warning sign or symptom

foreshadow to be a sign of future events

foresight the ability to judge and be prepared for future events

forestall to prevent or delay by acting first

foretell to indicate in advance; predict

forethought the ability to plan for the

future

forfeit to lose or give up something as a penalty or punishment

forfend to protect or preserve

forge to produce a fake copy; to set up, as an agreement; to move ahead in spite of difficulties

forgo to give up something; do without

forlorn sad and alone

formality observance of rules or customs; an established custom that may have no real importance

format the organization or arrangement of something

formative relating to growth or development

formidable causing fear; inspiring great respect; difficult to accomplish

formulaic done according to a fixed form

formulate to reduce to or express in a definite or set form

fornication sexual intercourse between two persons not married to each other

forsake to leave forever; to give up completely

forswear to give up or deny under oath

forte (for.TAY) an ability in which a person excels

forthcoming about to happen; (of a person) friendly and helpful

forthright direct and honest

fortify to strengthen

fortitude strength and courage in the face of difficulties

fortuitous happening by chance; fortunate

forum a place for the open exchange of ideas and information

foster to help to grow or develop

foulard a type of silk scarf or tie

founder to fall apart or fail

foursquare firm; forthright

fracas a noisy fight

fractious   rebellious; cranky

franchise   a right to sell a product or service within a given area; the right to vote in an election

frangible   easily broken

fraternal   of or like brothers; (of twins) not identical

fraternity   a grouping of people with common interests or occupations

fraternize   to mingle with others in a friendly way; to associate with an enemy or opposing group

fraudulent   dishonest; deceitful

fraught   filled with

fray   a quarrel or fight

freelance   to work as an independent, self-employed person

frenetic   wildly active or excited

fresco   a wall painting done on moist plaster

freshet   a stream of water that has suddenly risen

friable   easily crumbled

frieze   an ornamental band at the top of a wall

frippery   gaudy, ostentatious display in dress

frisson   a shiver of excitement or fear

frivolity   lighthearted fun

frivolous   silly or unimportant

frolic   to behave playfully

fructify   to bear fruit

frugal   careful about using money or resources; (of a meal) small and costing little

fruition   achievement of favorable results

fugitive   a person who flees, as from the law

fulcrum   the point on which a lever turns; a prop or support

fulgent   dazzlingly bright

fulgurant   flashing like lightning

fulminate to criticize or denounce strongly; (of an infection) to quickly increase in severity

fulsome excessive; insincere

fumigate to expose to chemical fumes in order to kill insects or disease

functional capable of working

functionary an official

funereal sad and suitable for a funeral

fungible (of goods) exchangeable or replaceable

furlough a leave of absence, esp. in the military

furor violent anger; uproar

further to help the progress of; advance

furtive done secretly or deceitfully

fusion the melting together of ideas or cultures

fusillade a continuous discharge of firearms

fustian a thick, rough cotton cloth

futile useless; hopeless

=G=

gadabout   a person who moves about a lot in social activities

gadfly   a person who stimulates or annoys with constant criticism

gaffe   an embarrassing social error

gainful   providing an income or advantage; profitable

gainsay   to declare to be untrue; contradict

gait   a way of walking or running

gall (n)   rudeness; nerve

gall (v)   to annoy

gallant   brave and noble

gallivant   to travel about in search of enjoyment

galvanize   to cause to act quickly

gambit   an action or remark intended to achieve a desired result

gambol   to run and jump playfully

game   ready and willing to try something new or difficult

gamut   the complete range

gander   the male of the goose; (slang) a look

gape   to stare in amazement, esp. with the mouth open; to open wide

garbled   (of something written or said) mixed up; confused

garçon   a restaurant waiter

garb   a style or type of clothing

gargantuan   of enormous size

gargoyle   an ugly stone figure usually in the shape of a strange animal's head

garish   too bright and showy

garner   to gather or acquire

garnish   to decorate food

garnishee   (in law) to attach wages in payment of a debt

garret   a small room at the top of a house

garrison the troops stationed at a military post

garrote to strangle with a rope or wire

garrulous too talkative

gastronomy the study of fine food and drink

gauche lacking social graces; tactless; awkward

gaudy too brightly colored and showy

gaunt very thin

gauntlet a heavy leather glove worn with armor; a challenge, as in to throw down or take up the gauntlet; a severe test or ordeal, as in to run the gauntlet

gawk to stare stupidly

gazebo a small, decorative structure in a garden

gazette a newspaper or periodical

geld to castrate an animal

gendarme a French police officer

genealogy a record of the descent of a family

generality a vague or imprecise statement

generalize to make a statement based on limited facts

generic (of a product) not having a trademark

genesis a beginning or origin

genetics the scientific study of the biological principles of heredity

genial cheerful and friendly

genitals the external sex organs

genocide the systematic destruction of a racial, religious, or cultural group

genome the complete set of genetic material of any living thing

genre a particular style or class of art, music, or literature

genteel polite and refined

gentile a person who is not Jewish

gentility good breeding; refinement

gentrification the improvement of a poor

housing area by middle class people who move there

gentry people of high social class

genuflect to bend the knee in respect

genus (in biology) a group of animals or plants ranking below a family and above a species

geocentric having the Earth as its center

geopolitics the study of how geography influences the politics of a country

geriatrics the medical study of the process of aging and the treatment of diseases of old age

germane connected with and important to a particular subject; pertinent

germinal being in the earliest stage of development

germinate to begin developing or growing

gerrymander to divide into political districts so as to give one party an advantage

gestalt a configuration that has qualities that are more than the sum of its parts

gestation the period during which the young develop in the uterus

gesticulate to make movements with the arms and hands while talking

ghastly terrifying or horrible; extremely unpleasant

ghetto a poor area of a city where a minority group lives

gibe a sarcastic remark

gig a job for a musician, as at a club

gigolo a man who provides romantic companionship for pay

gird to prepare for a difficult task

girth the measurement around a body or object; size or bulk

gist the central idea

glacial extremely slow; lacking friendliness or warmth

glaze (of the eyes) to become glassy, as

with boredom

glean to gather bit by bit

glib speaking or spoken quickly and easily without thought or sincerity

glom to grab; get hold of

gloss (n) a shiny appearance; an explanation or translation of a word

gloss (v) to cover over by hiding the truth

glossary an alphabetical list of terms with their definitions

glower to stare angrily

glut an oversupply

glutton a person who eats too much; a person who has a great capacity to tolerate something

gnash to grind the teeth together

gnome (in stories) a dwarf who lives underground and guards treasure

gnosis mystical knowledge

goad to push or urge

golem (in Jewish folklore) a figure made in the form of a man and given life

gonad a sexual organ that produces sperm or eggs

gonorrhea a sexually transmitted bacterial disease

gonzo outrageous; over the top

gory marked by bloodshed and violence

gossamer light and delicate

Gothic (of a type of literature) characterized by gloomy settings and mysterious or violent events

Gotterdammerung total downfall or destruction

gouge to overcharge

gourmand a person who enjoys eating large amounts of food

gourmet (goor.MAY) a connoisseur of food and drink

gradient the degree of change in a slope

graffiti drawings or writings on walls in public places

graft a surgical transplant of an organ or tissue; money or influence gained dishonestly

grandeur the quality of being impressive in size and beauty

Grand Guignol a short dramatic presentation employing sensationalism and horrific acts

grandiloquence extravagantly lofty or pompous speech

grandiose more complicated or impressive than is necessary

grant to give or allow; to concede or admit

graphic described in clear and vivid detail

grasping eager for money; greedy

gratis free of charge

gratuitous unnecessary and undeserved

gratuity a gift of money for service; a tip

gravitas seriousness and importance of manner

gravitate to be strongly attracted to

greening renewed freshness and vigor

gregarious sociable; friendly

gridlock a complete blockage of activity

grievance a wrong seen as good reason for complaint

grievous causing pain or suffering; very serious

grifter a dishonest gambler; swindler

grim stern or unyielding; cruel or forbidding

grisly causing horror or disgust

grist something used to one's advantage

grizzled having gray or partly gray hair

grotesque very strange or unnatural

grotto a small cave or cavern

groundless having no basis in fact

grouse to complain or grumble

grovel to behave in an extremely humble manner

grudgingly in an unwilling manner

guarded cautious; controlled

gubernatorial   pertaining to the office of state governor

guile   skillful deceit

guileless   innocent; straightforward

guise   outward appearance; false appearance

gulag   a forced labor camp, esp. for political prisoners

gullible   easily tricked or deceived

guru   a Hindu spiritual teacher; a leader or expert in a field

gustatory   pertaining to taste or tasting

guttural   pertaining to the throat or to a sound made in the back of the throat

gynecology   the branch of medicine that deals with disorders of the female reproductive system

gyrate   to move in a spiral or circular path

=H=

habeas corpus   a legal order requiring a person to be brought before a court of law as a protection against illegal imprisonment

haberdashery   a store that sells men's clothing and accessories

habitat   the area in which an animal or plant normally lives or grows

habitual   constant or usual

habitué   a frequent or usual visitor to a place

hack   a person, esp. a writer, who does routine work for hire and has low professional standards

hackles   the hairs that angry animals raise on the back of their necks

hackneyed   trite or stale through overuse

haggard   looking worn and exhausted

hagiography   an idealized biography; a biography of saints

halcyon   peaceful; happy

hale   healthy

halitosis   bad breath

hallowed   sacred; holy

hallucination   a perception of something that does not exist outside of the mind

halting   hesitant; uncertain

ham-handed   clumsy; inept

hamper   to prevent the progress or action of; hinder

hamstrung   made powerless or ineffective

handicap   to cause to be at a disadvantage

hanker   restless, incessant longing

hanky-panky   dishonest behavior

haphazard   by chance; random

hapless   unfortunate; unlucky

hara-kiri   a suicidal or self-destructive action; (Japanese) self-disembowelment by knife

harangue   a long, loud speech

harass   to annoy or criticize repeatedly

harbinger   a messenger or forerunner

harbor   to give shelter to; to hold in the mind, as a grudge

hardy   strong and healthy; able to survive harsh conditions

harebrained   foolish; stupid

hark   to listen; to refer back to past events

harlequin   a type of clown

harlot   a prostitute

harp   to repeat endlessly and annoyingly

harridan   a scolding, vicious woman; a shrew

harrowing   extremely upsetting

harry   to annoy or torment

hasten   to hurry

haughty   snobbish; arrogant

haute couture   (oht koo.TOOR)   high fashion

haute cuisine   (oht kwee.ZEEN)   gourmet cooking

hauteur   (oh.TUR)   snobbishness; arrogance

haut monde   (oht MAWND)   high society

havoc   great destruction

header   a plunge headfirst

headstrong   stubborn; willful

heady   intoxicating; exciting

heath   open land with small shrubs

heathen   a person considered to be uncivilized

heckle   to harass a public speaker with annoying remarks

hectic   full of intense activity or confusion

hector   to harass by bullying or scolding

hedge   to avoid giving a direct answer; to protect against financial loss by balancing one risk against another

hedonism   devotion to pleasure

heed   to pay attention to

heedless   paying little attention; reckless

hegemony   dominant influence or rule, as of one nation over others

hegira   a journey, esp. an escape to a more desirable place

heinous   very evil; monstrous

heir   a person who inherits the property or title of another

heirloom   a possession passed down from one generation to another

heist   an armed robbery

helix   a spiral

hellion   a wild, troublesome person

hemlock   a poisonous plant

hemophilia   an inherited disease in which the blood does not clot properly

hemorrhage   a large amount of bleeding

hemp   a plant grown for its tough fiber and as a source of marijuana

hence   therefore; from this time

henceforth   from now on

herald   a messenger or announcer of things to come

hereby   by this means; in this manner

heredity   the passing of characteristics from parents to offspring through genes

herein   in this

hereof   of this; concerning this

heresy   a belief that is contrary to accepted practice, esp. in religion

heretic   a person who does not conform to established opinions or practices

heretofore   before this time; until now

herewith   along with this

heritable   capable of being inherited

heritage   something passed down from previous generations

hermaphrodite   a plant, animal, or human being having reproductive organs of both sexes

hermeneutics   the study of the principles of interpretation, esp. of the Bible

hermetic sealed so that air cannot enter

hermitage a secluded place of residence

heterodox not in accordance with established beliefs

heterogeneous different in kind; not alike

heterosexual attracted to the opposite sex

heuristic encouraging learning through investigation and discovery

hew to cut with an axe; to adhere or conform

hiatus a gap, break, or interruption

hibernate to spend the winter in a deep sleep

hidebound rigid and inflexible in opinions and actions

hideous horribly ugly; disgusting

hierarchy organization by rank or social status

hieroglyph a picture or symbol of a word or idea

highbrow well-educated and cultured

high-flown unrealistic and extravagant

high-handed not considering the rights of others; overbearing

high-minded having noble ideals

high-toned elegant; stylish

hilarity boisterous cheerfulness or merriment

hilt the handle of a sword or dagger; the extreme

hinder to prevent or slow the progress of

hindmost at the farthest end; last

hindrance an obstacle or handicap

hindsight an understanding of the significance of an event after it has happened

hinterland a remote inland area

hireling a low-level employee who works only for pay

hirsute hairy

histrionic overly dramatic

hither to or toward here

hiterto until this time

hoary old and gray

hoax a deceptive trick or false report

hobble to restrain or handicap

hobnob to spend time together; socialize

hodgepodge a mixture of different things; a jumble

hogtie to prevent from acting; hamper

hoi polloi the common people

hokum complete nonsense

holdout a person who refuses to come to an agreement

holdover a person or thing left from the past

holistic an interacting whole entity that is more than the sum of its parts

holocaust total destruction, as by fire

holography a method of producing three-dimensional images by using a laser

homage special honor or respect

homeopathy a method of treating diseases by giving tiny amounts of substances that would produce the same symptoms as the disease

Homeric of heroic proportions; epic

homily an inspirational saying

homoerotic relating to or causing homosexual desire

homogeneous of the same or similar kind; uniform

homogenize to make uniform throughout

homonym a word that has the same sound and spelling as another word but differs in meaning

Homo sapiens human beings as a species

homosexual relating to or having sexual feelings for members of the same sex

homunculus a small human being

hone to sharpen or make more effective

honorarium a fee for services rendered by a professional person, as for a lecture

honorary given as an honor

honorific showing or giving honor or respect

hoodwink to deceive or mislead

hooligan a hoodlum or troublemaker

horizontal parallel to level ground

hormone any of various substances produced by the endocrine glands and carried in the bloodstream to organs and tissues in the body

hors de combat out of the fight

hors d'oeuvre (hor derve) a small bit of food served as an appetizer

hortatory urging to some course of action

horticulture the science of growing plants

hosanna a cry of praise or adoration

hospice a program providing supportive care for the terminally ill

hostel an inexpensive lodging place for travelers

hovel a small, dirty dwelling

hover to stay suspended in the air; to remain close by

hoyden a bold, carefree girl; a tomboy

hubbub noisy confusion

hubris (YOO.bris) arrogant pride

huff a state of anger or annoyance

humanism belief in human welfare and values

humanitarian a person devoted to human welfare and the advancement of social reforms

humanize to make humane

humanoid having human characteristics

humdrum dull; boring

humiliate to embarrass or shame

humility modesty; meekness

hummock a small hill or raised piece of ground

humor a state of mind; mood

hunker to hold firmly to one's opinions or actions

hurtle to move with great speed; plunge

husbandry the cultivation of crops and raising of livestock

hustings platforms where political speeches are made

hybrid a plant or animal that is a combination of different varieties or species

hygienic promoting good health; clean; sanitary

hymen a membrane that partly covers the opening of the vagina

hype exaggerated advertising claims or publicity

hyper overexcited; out of control

hyperbole a figure of speech in which exaggeration is used for dramatic effect

hypercritical overly or harshly critical

hypertension high blood pressure

hyperventilate to breathe abnormally fast

hypochondria a condition in which a person suffers from imaginary illnesses

hypocrisy the pretense of having beliefs or feelings that one does not actually hold

hypothesis a theory or assumption

hypothetical based on a theory; theoretical

hysterectomy surgical removal of the uterus

hysteria uncontrollable excitement or emotion

=I=

iatrogenic caused unintentionally by a physician or by medical treatment

icon a person who is greatly admired; a small image on a computer screen

iconoclast a person who criticizes widely held beliefs and traditions

id the part of the unconscious mind that is the source of the most basic human needs

idealist a person who believes in noble principles or goals

ideogram a written symbol that represents an idea or object

ideologue a person who believes very strongly in particular principles

ideology a set of beliefs or principles shared by members of a political or social group

idiom an expression whose meaning is different from the meanings of its individual words

idiopathic (of a disease) of unknown cause

idiosyncrasy a habit or characteristic that is peculiar to an individual

idiot savant a mentally defective person who exhibits exceptional skill in one field

idolatry the worship of idols

idyllic charmingly rustic and peaceful

ignoble of low character; base

ignominious humiliating; contemptible

ignominy disgrace; dishonor

ignoramus an extremely ignorant person

illegible very difficult to read

illicit unlawful; secretive

illimitable boundless

illiterate unable to read and write

illuminate to light; to make understandable

illuminati persons who claim superior

enlightenment

illusion a false impression; a mistaken idea

illusive deceiving

illusory misleading; unreal

illustrate to make clear with examples; to provide with pictures or diagrams

illustrious famous

imbecile a very stupid or foolish person

imbibe to drink, esp. alcoholic beverages

imbricate overlapping like shingles on a roof

imbroglio a very difficult and confusing situation

imbrue to stain

imbue to fill with a strong feeling

immaculate perfectly clean; flawless

immanent existing or occurring only within the mind; internal or subjective

immaterial of no importance

immemorial extending back beyond memory

immense huge and extensive size

immerse to cover completely with a liquid; to involve oneself deeply

immigrate to move to a foreign country to live

imminent about to happen

immobile not moving or not able to move

immoderate not usual or reasonable; extreme

immodest boastful or vain; showing too much of the body

immolate to kill oneself by burning, esp. as a protest

immoral against moral principles; sinful

immortal living forever

immune protected, as from disease or attack

immured closed away, as in prison

immutable unchangeable

impish mischievous

impale to pierce with a sharp object
impalpable difficult to feel or understand
impair to diminish in strength or quality; weaken or damage
impart to disclose; to give or bestow
impartial not favoring either side; unbiased
impasse a point at which no further progress is possible
impassive feeling or showing no emotion
impasto thickly laid-on paint
impeach to charge formally with misconduct in public office
impeccable having no flaws or faults
impecunious having very little money
impede to obstruct or hinder
impediment something that slows progress; a physical defect that prevents clear speech
impel to urge to action; drive
impending about to happen
impenetrable impossible to be entered or understood
impenitent feeling no regret about one's sins
imperative urgent or necessary; (in grammar) a command
imperceptible unable to be noticed or felt; very slight
imperialism a system in which one nation has economic and political dominance over other nations
imperil to put in danger
imperious having an attitude of superiority; arrogant
impermeable not permitting passage through
impermissible not allowed or permitted
impersonate to intentionally assume the characteristics or appearance of another
impertinent disrespectful; rude
imperturbable unshakably calm or

controlled

impervious not permitting passage, as of a liquid; incapable of being affected, as by criticism

impetuous characterized by hasty action, often without thought

impetus a driving or motivating force

impiety lack of respect for God or religion

impinge to have an effect on, often by limiting in some way

impious lacking reverence

implacable not able to be satisfied or changed

implausible hard to believe; not likely to be true

implement to put into effect; carry out

implication something implied or suggested; an indirect indication

implicit understood but not directly expressed

implode to collapse inward from some force

implore to beg urgently

impolitic not wise and likely to cause offense

imponderable not able to be guessed or estimated

import meaning; significance

importune to make repeated requests for something

imposing causing awe or admiration

impotence lack of strength or power; (of men) inability to have sexual intercourse

impound to seize and keep in legal custody

impoverished very poor

imprecation a swear word

impregnable so strong as to be impossible to attack or capture

impresario a manager or arranger of public entertainments, such as musical events

imprimatur official permission or approval

impromptu done without previous preparation

impropriety an inappropriate or unsuitable expression or act

improvident neglecting to provide for the future

improvise to perform without preparation; to construct from what is available

imprudent unwise; thoughtless

impudent rude and disrespectful

impugn to cast doubt upon, as someone's reputation

impunity freedom from risk of punishment

impute to attribute or ascribe, esp. something bad, to someone

in absentia in absence

inaccessible impossible or difficult to reach

inadmissible unacceptable in a court of law

inadvertent not meant or intended

inadvisable unwise

inalienable not able to be taken away

inamorata a female sweetheart or lover

inane lacking sense or meaning; stupid

inanimate lifeless; not moving

inapplicable not intended or suitable for a particular purpose

inappropriate not suitable or proper

inarticulate unable to speak or express oneself clearly

inaudible impossible to hear

inaugurate to install in public office with a formal ceremony

inauspicious not favorable or promising

inbred existing naturally from birth; resulting from breeding within a closely related group

incalculable too large to be counted;

limitless

in camera in the privacy of a judge's chambers

incandescent glowing; brilliant

incantation the chanting of words that cast a spell or perform magic

incapacitate to deprive of ability or strength; disable

incarcerate to put in jail

incarnate embodied in human form

incendiary able to cause fires; causing anger or conflict

incentive something that encourages action or greater effort

inception beginning; start

incessant continuing without stopping

incest sexual relations between close family members

inchoate not yet completely developed or formed

incidental minor or secondary

incinerate to burn to ashes

incipient just beginning

incisive sharp and clear

incite to stir up; provoke

inclement (of weather) stormy or rough

inclination natural tendency; preference

inclusive including everything

incognito with one's identity hidden or disguised

incoherent lacking logical connection; unable to make sense

incommodious inconvenient; uncomfortable

incommunicado not able or willing to communicate with others

incomparable finer than anything else in comparison

incompatible not able to live or work together harmoniously

incompetent lacking the necessary ability or qualification; incapable

incomprehensible impossible to understand

inconceivable hard to imagine

inconclusive leading to no clear answer or result; indefinite

incongruous not appropriate to the situation

inconsequential not important; trivial

inconsiderate thoughtless

inconsistent not in agreement; different from

inconsolable not able to be comforted

inconspicuous not obvious or noticeable

inconstant changeable; variable

incontestable not open to dispute; certain

incontinence inability to control the bladder or bowels

incontrovertible not open to question or dispute

incorporeal not having a physical body

incorrigible not capable of being corrected or reformed

incorruptible not subject to moral corruption

incredible unbelievable; extraordinary

incredulous withholding belief

increment an addition or increase

incriminate to show to be involved in a crime or fault

incubate to form or develop slowly, as an idea

incubus a demon said to have sexual intercourse with women while they are sleeping

inculcate to fix ideas or beliefs in someone's mind

incumbent currently holding a specified office

incur to become responsible for; to bring upon oneself

incursion a hostile entrance into a territory; a raid

indebted obligated to repay money or a kindness

indecent not in good taste; offensive

indecipherable not able to be read or understood

indecisive unable to make a decision; having no clear conclusion

indecorous behaving badly or rudely

indefatigable tireless

indefensible not able to be justified or excused

indelible impossible to remove; lasting

indelicate crude; tactless

indemnify to insure against possible loss or damage

indentured bound to work for another for a specified period of time, esp. as repayment

indeterminate not known or specified

index to adjust, as wages

indicative pointing out; expressing

indices numbers or formulas used for comparing values of things that vary against each other

indict to charge with wrongdoing

indifferent lacking in interest or feeling

indigenous native to a region or area

indigent poor; needy

indignant angered by something that is unfair or mean; offended

indignity something that offends a person's self-respect

indigo a dark violet-blue color

indiscreet not showing tact or good judgment

indiscriminate not showing careful thought or planning; not sorted or put in order

indispensable essential; necessary

indisposed slightly ill; unwilling

indisputable beyond doubt; unquestionable

indissoluble that cannot be dissolved; firm; binding

indistinct not easily seen or heard

individuate to give a distinctive character to

indivisible that cannot be divided or forced apart

indoctrinate to instruct in the teachings and beliefs of a particular group

indolent lazy

indomitable that which cannot be overcome or defeated; unconquerable

indubitable without doubt; certain

induce to persuade; to bring about

inducement a motive or incentive

induct to install as a member; to admit into military service

inductive using logical reasoning

indulge to humor or pamper; to yield to one's desires

indulgent lenient; yielding

industrious hard-working; diligent

inebriated drunk

inedible not fit to be eaten

ineffable incapable of being expressed or described

ineffectual not having the desired effect; useless

inefficacy lack of power to produce the desired effect

inefficient lacking in skill or ability

inelegant without grace; awkward

ineligible not qualified

ineluctable that which cannot be evaded; inescapable

inept awkward or clumsy; inappropriate

inequity lack of fairness

inerrant free from error

inert lacking the power to move or act

inertia resistance to action or motion

inestimable that cannot be estimated or fully appreciated

inevitable impossible to avoid or prevent

inexorable not capable of being stopped

inexplicable that cannot be explained or
understood

in extremis near death

inextricable unable to be disentangled or
escaped from

infallible incapable of error or failure

infamous well known for something bad or
shameful

infamy the condition of being shockingly
bad or evil

infantile lacking in maturity; childish

infatuation a strong but usually brief
feeling of love or attachment

infelicitous not apt or appropriate

infer to arrive at a conclusion based on
evidence

inference a conclusion

inferior low or lower in rank, quality, or
importance

infernal very bad or unpleasant

inferno a fiery place; hell

infertile unable to produce offspring

infest to trouble or invade in great numbers

infestation (of something bad) to be
present in large numbers

infidel one who does not believe in a
particular religion

infidelity unfaithfulness to one's spouse

infiltrate to join or enter secretly with
hostile intent

infinitesimal extremely small; minute

infinity a limitless space, period of time, or
number

infirmity physical weakness; frailty

inflammatory arousing strong emotions,
such as anger or hostility

inflection a change in the tone or sound of
the voice

inflexible rigid; unyielding

inflict to force to experience something unpleasant

influential by indirect having the power to produce effects on others means

influx an arrival of large numbers of people or things

infraction a breaking of a rule or law

infrastructure the basic foundation on which a system or community is built and which enables it to work, including facilities such as transportation and communication

infringe to violate a law or right; to intrude upon

infuriate to make very angry; enrage

infusion an inflow or addition

ingenious extremely clever and imaginative

ingenue (ON.zhuh.noo) the role of an innocent young woman in a play

ingenuous openly sincere and candid

ingest to eat or swallow

ingrained firmly fixed in the mind; deep-rooted

ingrate an ungrateful person

ingratiate to establish oneself in favor with another

ingress a means or place of entering

inhabitable able to be lived in or on

inhabitant a person who lives in a certain place

inherent being a natural or basic part of a person or thing

inhibit to hold back or prevent

inhospitable not welcoming; unfriendly

inhumane lacking kindness or compassion

inimical having a bad effect; harmful

inimitable impossible to copy; unique

iniquity extreme injustice or wickedness

initial relating to or occurring at the beginning; first

initiate to begin or start

initiative   the first step; ability to begin
   action
injudicious   showing poor judgment;
   unwise
injunction   an order from a court of law
inkling   a vague idea; a hint or clue
in loco   in the place of
in loco parentis   in the place of a parent
in medias res   in the middle of things
in memoriam   in memory of
inkling   a vague idea; a hint or clue
innate   possessed at birth; being an
   essential characteristic
innocuous   harmless; innocent
innovation   something newly improved or
   introduced
innuendo   an indirect hint intended to
   damage a person's reputation
innumerable   too numerous to count
inoculate   to inject with a vaccine
inopportune   coming at a bad time
inordinate   more than necessary; excessive
inquest   a legal investigation into the cause
   of a death
inquiry   a question; a request for
   information
inquisitive   asking lots of questions; curious
inroads   progress toward or into something
insatiable   impossible to satisfy; never
   having enough
inscrutable   not easily understood;
   mysterious
inseminate   to make pregnant
insensate   without feeling or sensitivity
inseparable   impossible to separate
insidious   harmful in a gradual and secret
   way
insight   ability to see or know the truth
insinuate   to hint slyly about something bad
insipid   lacking flavor; lacking exciting

qualities

insistence   strong pressure to do something

in situ   in place

insolent   disrespectfully bold; rude

insoluble   not able to be solved

insolvent   unable to pay one's debts

insomnia   inability to sleep

insouciant   free of care or concern; indifferent; nonchalant

instigate   to make something happen; provoke

instill   to introduce gradually, as into the mind

institute   to establish or set in operation; begin

nsubordinate   disrespectful to authority

insubstantial   lacking substance or reality; not strong or solid

insufferable   extremely annoying; unbearable

insular   isolated; alone

insuperable   impossible to overcome or surmount

insupportable   unbearable

insure   to make certain

insurgent   rising in revolt

insurmountable   impossible to overcome

insurrection   a revolt or rebellion

intangible   not able to be seen or felt and therefore difficult to explain or show

integer   any positive or negative whole number or zero

integral   necessary; essential

integrate   to bring all groups together into a whole

integrity   moral strength; completeness

intellectual   a highly educated person whose interests involve careful thinking and mental effort

intelligentsia   the highly educated and cultured people in a society

intelligible   capable of being understood

intemperate out of control

intensive concentrated; deep

intent firmly fixed on some purpose; determined

intention a purpose or plan

inter to put in a grave; bury

interact to communicate with or react to each other

intercede to act on behalf of someone

intercourse the act of having social or sexual relations

interdict to forbid; prohibit

interface the point at which two systems interact, esp. the connection between two electronic devices

interim an interval of time between two events

interject to make a comment while someone else is speaking

interlocutory pertaining to or occurring in conversation

interloper a person who intrudes into the affairs of others

intermediate being between or in the middle

interment burial

interminable seemingly endless

intermittent stopping and starting repeatedly

intern a person who is finishing training for a skilled job, esp. in medicine

internecine involving conflict or struggle within a group

internment confinement, as for prisoners of war

interpolate to add information to a written work

interpose to put in the middle of, as a remark

interregnum an interval of time between the reign of two rulers

interrogate to question a person formally

and thoroughly

interrogative or **interrogatory** expressing a question

intersect to cross each other, as two roads

intersperse to scatter at intervals among other things

interstices very small cracks or spaces

intertwine to wind around each other

interval a pause in time

intervene to come between in order to prevent or change a course of events

intestate (in law) without a will at death

intimate to hint or imply

intimidate to make fearful or timid, as by threats

intolerable impossible to bear

intolerant not willing to accept different beliefs, opinions, or groups

intonation the rise and fall in pitch of the speaking voice

in toto completely; entirely

intoxication drunkenness

intractable difficult or impossible to manage or control

intramural involving members of the same school or institution

intransigent refusing to compromise or be persuaded

intravenous an injection into a vein; within a vein

intrench to establish firmly or securely

intrepid brave; fearless

intricate having a complicated structure; hard to understand or solve

intrigue (n) a secret plot or scheme; crafty dealings

intrigue (v) to excite the interest or curiosity of

intrinsic belonging to the basic nature of a thing

intromit to put in or let in; admit

introspection examination of one's own

thoughts and emotions

introvert a person whose thoughts and feelings are primarily directed inward rather than toward the social environment

intrude to enter without permission

intuition an immediate understanding or feeling about something without reasoning or proof

inundate to overwhelm, as if with a flood

inure to toughen or harden, as by exposure

invalidate to make illegal or unusable

invariable unchanging; constant

invective insulting or abusive speech

inveigh to protest or criticize strongly

inveigle to entice or acquire by artful persuasion

inverse opposite or reversed

invert to turn upside down

investiture a ceremony in which someone is given an official rank or authority

inveterate confirmed in a habit or practice; firmly established

invidious causing resentment or envy

invigorate to fill with energy; stimulate

invincible too strong to be defeated or overpowered

in vino veritas in wine there is truth

inviolable that must not or cannot be broken, damaged, or doubted

in vitro developed in an artificial environment in a laboratory, as in a test tube

invocation an opening prayer

invoice an itemized bill for goods or services

invoke to call upon for help; to appeal to for confirmation

invulnerable not able to be attacked or damaged

iota a tiny amount

ipse dixit he himself said it

ipso facto by the fact itself

irascible   easily angered or irritated

irate   very angry

ire   anger

iridescent   displaying shiny colors of the rainbow

irksome   annoying; irritating

ironic   contrary to what was expected or intended; expressing the opposite of what is actually meant

irony   a sometimes odd difference between what exists and what might have been expected

irradiate   to expose to radiation

irrational   lacking sound judgment; not guided or controlled by reason

irreconcilable   not able to be brought together in agreement

irredeemable   not able to be corrected or improved

irreducible   not able to be reduced or simplified

irrefutable   not able to be disproved; definitely true

irrelevant   having no relation to the situation; not applicable

irremediable   impossible to correct or cure

irreparable   impossible to repair or set right

irreplaceable   impossible to replace; unique

irrepressible   incapable of being restrained or controlled

irreproachable   free from blame or fault

irresolute   lacking firm purpose

irrespective   regardless

irretrievable   impossible to get back; unrecoverable

irreverent   showing a lack of respect, esp. for religious beliefs

irreversible   impossible to put back to original form

irrevocable   that cannot be changed or

undone

irritable easily annoyed or disturbed

irritant something that causes annoyance or makes a physical condition worse

isolate to set apart from others

isometric involving contraction of muscles with little movement

isthmus a narrow strip of land with water on each side which connects two larger areas of land

iterate to say again or repeatedly

itinerant traveling from place to place or job to job

itinerary a detailed list of places to visit during a trip

ivory tower a situation, attitude, or place away from worldly, practical affairs

=J=

jaded tired or worn out; dulled by overindulgence

jape a joke or trick

jargon the specialized vocabulary peculiar to a trade, profession, or group

jaundiced showing or influenced by distaste or hostility

jaunt a short pleasure trip

jaunty having a happy and confident manner; stylish in appearance

jeer to shout or laugh mockingly

jejune lacking interest or maturity; very simple or childish

jeremiad a prolonged complaint

jerry-built built hastily and poorly

jettison to throw something away, as off a ship or aircraft

jezebel a wicked, deceitful woman

jibe (n) a sarcastic remark

jibe (v) to be the same; agree

jihad a holy war or vigorous crusade

jilt to end a relationship with a lover abruptly

jingoism belligerent patriotism

jobber a wholesale merchant

jocose joking; playful

jocular tending to make jokes; meant as a joke

jocund cheerful; merry

joie de vivre (jwah duh VEEV.ruh) enjoyment of living

jostle to push, esp. in a crowd of people

joust to compete for control

jovial jolly; cheerful

jubilant full of great joy

judas a person who betrays a friend

judgmental making moral judgments

judiciary the system of courts of law and

judges

judicious   showing good judgment; wise

juggernaut   an overpowering, unstoppable force

jugular   pertaining to or located in the neck or throat, as the jugular vein that returns blood from the head to the heart

juncture   a point in time, esp. a turning point

junket   a trip made by a government official at public expense

junta   a group of military officers who have taken power in a country by force

jurisdiction   authority or control

jurisprudence   the study of law

justify   to give or to be a good reason for

juxtapose   to place side by side for comparison

=K=

kafkaesque senselessly complex and strangely menacing, as in a nightmare

kaleidoscopic quickly changing from one thing to another

kamikaze reckless and suicidal

kaput finished; unable to function

karaoke an electronic device that provides an instrumental accompaniment for a singer

karma fate or destiny; cause and effect

keen (adj) intelligent; sharp; intense

keen (v) to bewail or lament the dead

keep board and lodging; the central tower or dungeon of a medieval castle

ken knowledge or understanding

keynote the main idea or theme, as of a speech

khaki a heavy, yellowish brown cloth

kibitz to offer advice or criticism

kibbutz a community farm in Israel

kindle to arouse or excite

kindred belonging to the same family or group

kinetic relating to or produced by motion

kingpin the most important person in a field or organization

kinky peculiar or unusual, esp. regarding sexual activity

kiosk a small structure where newspapers or other items are sold

kismet fate; destiny

kith acquaintances; friends

kitsch cheap decorative objects of poor quality

klatsch a casual gathering

kleptomania an uncontrollable urge to steal

klutz a clumsy person

knave a dishonest, untrustworthy man

knead to press with the fingers and hands

knell the sound of a bell rung slowly, esp. for a death

knoll a small rounded hill or mound

kosher proper; legitimate; clean

kowtow to show too much respect or obedience to someone in authority

kudos praise; acclaim

kvetch to complain

Kwanza an African-American harvest festival celebrated from December 26 to January 1

=L=

labyrinth   a complicated or bewildering arrangement or state of things; a maze

lacerate   to rip or tear roughly

lachrymose   mournful; tearful

lackadaisical   lacking spirit or interest

lackey   a follower who behaves like a servant

lackluster   lacking brightness or interest; ordinary or dull

laconic   using few words; concise

lactate   to produce milk

lacuna   a gap or missing part

laggard   moving or developing slowly; sluggish

lagniappe   (lan.YAP)   a small gift or gratuity

laissez-faire   (lay.say.FAIR)   an economic policy that opposes government regulation of free enterprise

laity   religious worshipers who are not part of the clergy

lambaste   to criticize strongly

lambent   shining softly; clever and playful, as wit

lament   to express grief or regret for

lamentable   deserving sorrow or regret

laminate   to join together thin layers of material

lampoon   to attack with humor or ridicule

landsman   one who lives on the land and knows little of seamanship; (Jewish) someone from the same country

languid   lacking energy or spirit

languish   to become weak or feeble; to suffer neglect or hardship, as in prison

languor   a pleasantly lazy mood or quality

lanky   tall, thin, and awkward

lapidary   a person who works with

precious stones

lapse   to fail, slip, or sink; to be no longer valid, as a subscription

larceny   the stealing of property

larder   a place for storing food; a pantry

largess or **largesse**   generous giving of gifts

lascivious   expressing or feeling lust; lewd

lassitude   lack of energy; tiredness

latent   present but not active; dormant

lateral   on or to the side

latitude   freedom to act; distance north or south of the equator

latter   nearer the end; later

laud   to praise highly

laudable   praiseworthy

laudatory   expressing praise

laureate   a person who has been honored with an award for achievement

laurels   honors won for achievement

lave   to wash

lavish   done in generous amounts

lax   lacking strict control or attention

lay   not expert in a field; not of the clergy

leaden   heavy or dull

leaven   to improve by making livelier; adding yeast to bread dough

lecherous   lustful; erotically suggestive

lectern   a stand for papers from which to give a speech

leery   suspicious; cautious

legacy   something passed on by an earlier generation

legation   a group of officials who represent their government in a foreign country

legerdemain   trickery; the practice of stage magic; deception

legible   capable of being read

legislate   to make or pass laws

legume   a plant that has its seeds in a pod, as beans and peas

leitmotif   a theme that runs through a piece

of music or work of art

leonine like a lion

leper a person who is rejected or shunned;
a victim of leprosy

lesbian a homosexual woman

lesion a localized area of injured, diseased,
or abnormal tissue

lest for fear that

lethal able to cause death; deadly

lethargic lacking in energy; drowsy or
sluggish

Levant the lands bordering the eastern
shores of the Mediterranean Sea

leviathan something that is extremely large
and powerful

levitate to rise or cause to rise in the air
and float

levity lack of appropriate seriousness;
frivolity

levy to impose or collect a tax

lewd obscene; indecent

lexicographer an author of dictionaries

lexicon a dictionary; a set of words in a
particular field

liable legally responsible; likely to do or
experience

liaison a connection maintained by
communication between units of an
organization; a love affair

libation a drink of wine or other alcoholic
beverage

libel something that unjustly damages a
person's reputation

liberal generous; (in politics) proposing
change; progressive

liberal arts college studies that provide
general knowledge, as in the humanities
and natural sciences

liberate to set free

libertarian one who advocates liberty and
free will; a political party which calls for
very little government

libertine a person who is morally and sexually unrestrained

libido sexual drive

libidinous lustful; lewd

libretto the text of an opera or musical

license legal permission; freedom of action

licentious sexually unrestrained

liege a feudal lord; a loyal subject

lien a legal claim on property as payment for a debt

lieu in place of

lilliputian extremely small; tiny

lilt a pleasant, rhythmic quality in a person's voice

limbo a state of uncertain waiting; a condition of neglect or oblivion

limelight the center of public attention

limn to outline or describe

limpid perfectly clear; transparent

linchpin something very important that holds different parts together and keeps them functioning

lineage ancestry

lineaments distinguishing features or details

linear relating to a line or to length; direct or connected

lingam a representation of the male phallus in Hindu cosmology

lingerie women's underclothes

lingo language of a special group

lingua franca any of various languages widely used as a means of communication and commerce among speakers of diverse languages

linguistics the study of the nature and structure of language

lionize to treat as a celebrity

lip-sync to match lip movements to recorded sound

liquefy to make or become liquid

liqueur a sweet alcoholic drink

liquidate   to sell off or get rid of; to close a business; to kill

liquidity   the condition of being easily converted to cash

lissome   agile and graceful

litany   a ceremonial form of prayer; a long, tedious account, as of complaints

literal   corresponding word for word; following the exact meaning of a word; factual

literary   relating to literature or the profession of writing

literate   able to read and write; well-educated

literati   scholarly or intellectual persons as a group

lithe   able to move and bend easily; limber

litigant   a person involved in a legal action

litigate   to carry on a lawsuit

litigious   inclined to litigate or to dispute

litmus test   a figurative test in which a single factor is the deciding issue

litotes   understatement

liturgy   the established form for a church service

livery   a special uniform worn by servants

livid   extremely angry; pale, esp. from anger

loath   not willing; reluctant

loathe   to dislike greatly; detest

lobby   to try to influence lawmakers in regard to special interests

lobotomize   to make someone abnormally tranquil by destroying tissue in the cerebral cortex of the brain

locale   a particular place; a scene or setting for a play or film

lockstep   a rigidly inflexible set of rules

locution   a manner or style of speaking

lode   a deposit of metal, esp. silver or gold

lofty   elevated; noble

loggerheads   disagreement

logistics coordination, planning, and implementation of the details of a business or other operation

longevity long life

longitude position to the east or west of an imaginary line on the Earth's surface

longueurs a boring period of time

lop to cut off a part

lope to run in an easy, graceful way

loquacious tending to talk too much

lore stories, customs, and beliefs on a particular subject

lorgnette a pair of eyeglasses mounted on a handle

lothario a man who seduces women

louche disreputable; indecent

lout a stupid, boorish person

lowbrow uncultured; common

lubricious arousing sexual desire; marked by lechery

lubricity oily smoothness; lewdness

lucent marked by clarity; translucent

lucid clearly understood; mentally sound

lucrative producing wealth; profitable

lucre money or profit

Luddite one who opposes new technologies

ludicrous ridiculous; absurd

lugubrious sorrowful; mournful

lumber to walk in a heavy, clumsy manner

luminary a person highly respected for achievement in a field

luminous full of light; intellectually brilliant

lummox a stupid, clumsy person

lumpen pertaining to the lowest class of society

lunacy insanity

lunar relating to the moon

lunatic an insane person

lurid causing shock or horror

luscious juicy and delicious

lush (adj) richly abundant

lush (n) a person who is often drunk

lust intense sexual desire

luster shine or gloss; glory or splendor

lustrous shining

luxuriant growing abundantly

luxurious providing great comfort and pleasure

lyceum an educational institution

lyrical (of poetry) expressing personal thoughts and feelings; (of music) expressing warmth and emotion

lyricist a person who writes words for songs

=M=

macabre suggesting death and decay; gruesome; ghastly

macadam compacted broken stone used for paving

macerate to soften by steeping in a liquid

Machiavellian characterized by the use of unscrupulous means to gain power

machinations secret methods used to trick others

machismo an exaggerated sense of manliness or power

macho (of men) excessively tough and virile

macrocosm a huge system, such as the world or the universe

maculate stained; impure

madcap foolishly impulsive

madding noisy and disorderly

mademoiselle the French equivalent of Miss

madrigal a short lyric poem

maelstrom a violent whirlpool; a very dangerous situation

maestro a famous conductor of music; a master of any art

Mafia a secret organization involved in criminal activities

magistrate a government official with the authority to administer the law, as a judge

magna cum laude with high academic honors

magnanimous generous and honorable

magnate a person of great influence and importance, esp. in business or industry

magnificent very impressive in appearance; splendid; remarkable

magnitude greatness of size or amount

magnum opus the chief work of a writer

or artist

maim to disable by causing the loss of use of an arm or leg; to impair or disfigure

mainstay a person or thing which acts as a chief support

maitre d' a headwaiter in a restaurant

major domo a man in charge of a large household, as a palace

maladjusted poorly adapted to one's circumstances

maladroit awkward or unskilled

malady a disease or disorder

malaise a vague sense of illness or discomfort; an unhealthy condition

malapropism the amusing misuse of a word in place of another that sounds similar

malarkey meaningless or misleading talk

malcontent a dissatisfied or rebellious person

mal de mer seasickness

malediction a curse

malefaction an evil deed; wrongdoing

malefactor a criminal

malefic producing evil; causing harm

maleficent evil or harmful

malevolent wishing harm to others; malicious

malfeasance dishonest or illegal behavior, esp. by a person in authority

malice a wish to harm others; harmful intent

malicious mean; spiteful

malign to speak harmful untruths about; slander

malignant inclined to cause harm; (of a tumor) cancerous

malinger to pretend to be ill in order to avoid work

malleable easily controlled or influenced

malodorous having a bad odor

malpractice improper treatment by a

professional, esp. a physician

maltreat   to treat cruelly

manacles   handcuffs

mandarin   a powerful government official or bureaucrat

mandate   the authority given to an elected group of people to perform an action or govern a country; a written order or command

mandatory   required; obligatory

maneuver   a planned and controlled movement or procedure

mania   a mental disorder marked by extreme agitation; an intense enthusiasm

maniacal   wild; uncontrolled

Manichaean   the struggle between the forces of light and dark, with dark regarded as evil

manifest   to show clearly through signs or symptoms

manifestation   the showing or proving of something

manifesto   a public statement of the political or economic aims of a group

manifold   of many kinds

manipulate   to operate or handle something, esp. with skill; to manage or influence, esp. for one's own advantage

mannequin   a full-sized plastic or plaster model of the human body used for displaying clothes

mannerism   a distinctive personal gesture or habit

manor   the main house on an estate

manqué   (mahn.KAY)   unfulfilled; unsuccessful

mantra   an often-repeated word or phrase that sometimes expresses a belief or desire

marauding   roving in search of plunder; acting to steal and destroy

marginal   barely acceptable; of little

importance

marginalize to put in a position of little importance or influence

marital pertaining to marriage

maritime relating to the sea

marmoreal of or like marble

martial relating to war or the military

martinet a person who stubbornly demands strict adherence to rules and orders

martyr a person who suffers greatly, esp. for a cause

masochism gratification, esp. sexual pleasure, derived from pain or discomfort inflicted by another

masquerade a disguise or false pretense

massacre a slaughter of many people or animals

masseur a man who gives massages professionally

masseuse a woman who gives massages professionally

masterstroke an extremely clever and successful action

mastery the ability to do something extremely well; great skill

masthead a box or column that shows the names of the owners, editors, and staff members of a newspaper or magazine

masticate to chew food

masturbation sexual stimulation of one's own genitals

materialism the belief that accumulating money and possessions is the major goal in life

materiel all the equipment and supplies used by an organization, esp. the military

maternal related to a mother or motherhood

matriarch the female head of a family or society

matricide the killing of one's mother

matriculate to enroll officially as a student in a college or university

matrix an arrangement of quantities in columns and rows; the place or point from which something originates

maudlin overly or embarrassingly sentimental

maul to injure or damage by rough treatment

maunder to talk in a rambling way; to wander

mausoleum a large burial tomb

mawkish very sentimental; maudlin

maxim a brief saying that states a basic principle

mayhem a state of uncontrolled violence or disorder

mea culpa my fault; a formal expression of guilt

meander to follow a winding path; to wander about

measured careful; deliberate

meddlesome inclined to interfere in the affairs of others

media (sing. **medium**) journalists or news organizations as a group

median dividing in two equal parts; the middle

mediate to help opposing sides resolve their differences

medieval extremely old-fashioned or primitive; pertaining to the Middle Ages

mediocre neither good nor bad; second-rate

meditate to engage in deep and quiet thought

medley a mixture or variety

megalith a stone of great size

megalomania delusional ideas of grandeur and power

megalopolis a very large city or urban region

meister a master or expert

melancholy sadness or depression

mélange a mixture

meld to merge or blend

melee (may.lay) a disorderly fight among several people

meliorate to make better or less bad

mellifluous sweetly flowing, as a voice

melodramatic emotional or sentimental in an exaggerated manner

memento an object that is a reminder of the past

memento mori an object that serves as a reminder of death

memoirs a type of autobiography

memorabilia objects from the past that are worth remembering; souvenirs

memorandum an informal, written message used within an organization

menace to threaten or endanger

menage a domestic establishment

ménage à trois (men.azh ah TWAH) a domestic arrangement in which three people live together in a sexual relationship

menagerie a collection of wild animals; a strange group of people

mendacious telling lies

mendacity untruthfulness

mendicant a beggar

menial referring to humble or degrading tasks

mensch a person who is decent and responsible

menses menstrual flow

menstruation the monthly discharge of blood and tissue from the uterus

mentor a wise and trusted teacher and friend

mercantile related to merchants or trade

mercenary (adj) concerned mainly with money; greedy

mercenary (n) a soldier for hire

mercurial changeable; unstable

meretricious seeming attractive but of little value; based on pretense

meringue a mixture of whipped egg whites, sugar, and flavoring used as a topping for desserts

meritorious deserving praise

merits the rights and wrongs of a matter

mesmerize to fascinate or hypnotize

mesomorph a person of medium size

messiah an expected savior or deliverer

metabolism the physical and chemical processes in the body that supply energy and make growth possible

metamorphosis a complete change in character or appearance

metaphor a figure of speech in which a word or phrase associated with one thing is used of another to suggest a comparison

metaphysics the branch of philosophy that studies the nature of reality and knowledge

metastasize (of cancer) to spread from one part of the body to another

mete to distribute or dispense

meteorology scientific study of the weather

methodical done in a careful, systematic manner

methodology a system of methods and principles used in a particular discipline

meticulous extremely thorough and precise; giving great attention to details

metier one's occupation or specialty

metropolis a large, important city

metropolitan characteristic of a large city or its inhabitants; sophisticated

mettle courage and endurance; character

miasma a heavy, vaporous fog; an unpleasant, foreboding influence or atmosphere

microcosm a small, complete version of something much larger

microorganism any living thing that can be seen only under a microscope

micturate to urinate

middlebrow a moderately cultured person

middling moderate or average in size or quality

midriff the middle part of the human body

midst a position among or with others

mien a person's appearance or facial expression

migraine a severe headache that occurs repeatedly in some people

migrate to move from one place to another

migratory traveling from one place to another at regular times, as birds

milestone an important event

milieu environment; surroundings

militant aggressive or ready to fight, esp. in support of a cause

militarism the policy of maintaining a large and powerful military establishment

militate to weigh heavily against

militia a body of citizen soldiers called out in times of emergency

millennium a period of one thousand years

milquetoast a timid person

mime to imitate actions and moods without speaking

mimic to imitate or copy, as in speech or mannerisms, esp. in order to ridicule

minaret a tall, thin tower attached to a mosque

minatory threatening; menacing

mince to walk with small, delicate steps; (of words) to make words less direct and disturbing

mingy stingy

minimal smallest in amount or degree

minimize to lessen; to make something seem smaller or less important

minion a servile follower or underling

minister (n) a member of the clergy; a person in charge of a department of the government

minister (v) to attend to another's person's needs

minority a racial, ethnic, religious, or political group that is different from the majority of people in a country

minstrel in medieval times, a traveling musician and singer

mint (n) a place where the coins of a country are made

mint (adj) in new and undamaged condition

minuet a slow, graceful 17th-century dance

minuscule very small; tiny

minutiae small details

mirabile dictu wonderful to relate

mirage an illusion of something far away that does not exist

mire to hold or trap, as if in mud

misadventure an unlucky experience

misalliance a connection, as between nations, that does not work well

misandry hatred of men

misanthrope a person who dislikes other people

misapprehend to fail to understand correctly

misappropriate to steal or embezzle

misbegotten illegitimate

miscegenation marriage between a man and woman of different races

mischance bad luck

mischievous playfully or slyly annoying

misconception a mistaken idea

misconstrue to mistake the meaning of

miscreant someone who behaves badly

misdemeanor   a minor legal offense

mise-en-scène   the stage setting of a play

misnomer   a wrong name or label

misogamy   hatred of marriage

misogyny   hatred of women

missive   a letter or document

mitigate   to make less severe

mnemonic   relating to the memory

mobilize   to assemble for a particular purpose, as for war

mockery   ridicule; an offensive or ridiculous imitation

modality   an attribute that denotes mode of procedure or manner of taking effect

modicum   a small amount

modish   stylish; fashionable

modulate   to change the level, strength, or tone of

modus operandi   method of working or operating

modus vivendi   way of life; lifestyle

mogul   a very rich or powerful person

moil   to work hard

mollify   to lessen the anger of

mollycoddle   to pamper

molt   (of animals) to shed an outer covering, as skin or feathers

molten   melted by great heat

momentous   greatly significant

momentum   force or speed of movement, as of a physical object or the development of events

monad   a single unit or entity

monarch   a hereditary ruler, as a king or queen

monastery   a place where monks live

monastic   relating to the simple lifestyle of monks

monetary   relating to money

monger   a person who is involved in a petty activity that causes trouble, as a rumor-monger

moniker   a name or nickname

monitory   serving as a warning

monochromatic consisting of a single color

monogamy   the practice of having only one spouse at a time

monograph   a long article that deals with a subject extensively

monolith   a large single block of stone; something that is massive and inflexible

monologue   a long educational, dramatic or comic piece spoken by a single performer

monomania   an obsessive interest in a single thing

monopolize   to get or have control over

monopoly   sole possession or control of something

monosyllabic   consisting of one syllable

monotheism   belief that there is only one God

monotone   a boring sameness, as of sound or color

monotony   boring sameness or repetition

monsoon   a heavy rain storm, esp. of southeast Asia

montage   a piece of work produced by combining elements from different sources

monumental   impressively large, long-lasting, or important

moor   to secure, as a boat, with lines or anchors

moot   open to discussion; no longer relevant

morale   the level of enthusiasm or confidence of a person or group

morality   virtuous conduct in human behavior or relationships

moralize   to express judgments about matters of right and wrong

morass   a swampy area; a very difficult or confusing situation

moratorium a temporary pause or ban

morbid relating to thoughts of death or decay; relating to disease

mordant biting; sarcastic

mores (MORE.aze) customs and rules of behavior of a social group

moribund near death

morose gloomily ill-humored

morsel a small portion of tasty food

mortality the condition of being subject to death

mortician a funeral director

mortify to cause to feel shame or embarrassment

mosaic a picture or design made of small colored pieces, as of glass or stone

mosque a Muslim house of worship

mote a small particle or speck, as of dust

motif a theme or design that is used repeatedly in a work of art, music or literature

mot juste (moh zhoost) the exactly right word

motley made up of greatly varied elements or colors

mottled spotted or streaked with different colors

mountebank an unscrupulous pretender; a person who sells quack medicines

moxie courage and boldness

mucilage glue

muckrake to search for and expose scandals about public officials

mudslinging efforts to discredit a political opponent with malicious statements

muffle to lower the sound of

mufti civilian clothes worn by someone who usually wears a uniform

mulatto a person of mixed black and white ancestry

mulct to defraud or swindle

mulish stubborn

multifaceted having many sides or aspects

multifarious numerous and varied

multiform having many shapes or kinds

multilingual using or able to use several different languages

multiplicity a great number or variety

multitude a large number, esp. of people

mundane commonplace; ordinary; dull

munificent displaying great generosity

muse (n) inspiration, as for a poet or artist

muse (v) to think about something carefully for a long time

musky having a strong, animal odor

muster to gather or summon up, as an emotion or support

mutable subject to change or alteration

mutant a living thing that is different from others of its type because of a permanent genetic change

mutilate to damage severely, esp. by cutting off a necessary part

mutinous rebellious; uncontrolled

mutter to speak in low, unclear tones

muzzle to restrain from speech

myopic near-sighted; unable to plan ahead

myriad a vast number

mystical having a meaning that is beyond human comprehension

mysticism a religion based on mystical communion with an ultimate reality or God

mystique an aura of special power or mystery surrounding a person or thing

=N=

nabob a very wealthy or powerful person

nacreous pearly

nadir the lowest or worst point

naif an inexperienced person

naive showing a lack of experience or judgment

naiveté childlike simplicity

nanosecond one billionth of a second

narcissism excessive self-love; vanity

nascent coming into existence

natal relating to birth

nativism a policy of favoring native inhabitants as opposed to immigrants

natter to talk continuously

naught zero; nothing

nautical relating to ships, sailors, or navigation

nave the long central part of a church

navigate to steer vehicle, as a ship or airplane

naysayer a person who is always negative or pessimistic

neanderthal very old-fashioned and reactionary

nebbish a pitifully inept and timid person

nebulous cloudlike; hazy; indistinct

necessitate to make necessary or unavoidable

necromancy a method of predicting the future by communicating with the dead

necrophilia sexual attraction to dead bodies

necrosis death of a localized part of living tissue

nee born (used before the maiden name of a married woman)

neer-do-well an idle, worthless person

nefarious evil; wicked

negate   to cause to be ineffective or useless; invalidate

negligee   a woman's sheer dressing gown or robe

negligence   failure to act with care or concern

negligible   too slight to be of importance

nemesis   a source of great difficulty or harm; an unbeatable opponent

neologism   a new word or expression

neophyte   a beginner or novice

ne plus ultra   the highest point that can be attained

nepotism   favoritism shown to relatives in the workplace

nether   located below

netherworld   the infernal regions; hell

nettle   to irritate or provoke

neurasthenia   a nervous disorder characterized by chronic fatigue, persistent pains, and depression

neurosis   a mental illness characterized by anxiety, obsession, or depression

neurotic   a person who is unreasonably nervous or anxious

neuter (adj)   neither masculine nor feminine in grammatical gender

neuter (v)   to castrate or spay an animal

neutralize   to prevent or counteract the effect of

nexus   a connected series or group; the core or center of a system

niche   a situation that is exactly suited to a person

niggardly   stingy; ungenerous

niggling   petty; trivial

nigh   near; approaching

nihilism   a system of thought that holds that all principles or beliefs are meaningless and existence is senseless

nil   nothing; zero

nimble   quick and clever

nimbus   a cloud or aura surrounding a person or thing

nirvana   an ideal condition of great happiness and contentment

nitty-gritty   the specific or practical details

nob   a rich and important person

noblesse oblige   (o.bleejh)   the moral obligation of persons with wealth and influence to help others

nocent   harmful

nocturnal   relating to or happening at night

node   a lump or swelling on or in living tissue; a device within a computer network

noetic   relating to the mind

noisome   bad-smelling; harmful to one's health

nomadic   wandering from place to place

nom de guerre   (duh GARE)   an assumed name; pseudonym

nom de plume   a fictitious name used by an author; pen name

nomenclature   the system of names used in science or other fields

nominal   very small, as a sum of money; in name only

nominate   to propose as a candidate for election; to appoint to an office

nonce   for the present moment or purpose; (of a word) invented for a particular occasion or situation

nonchalant   carefree and unconcerned

noncommittal   indefinite about a decision or opinion

noncompliance   failure to obey a law

non compos mentis   not of sound mind

nonconformist   one who does not behave according to generally accepted standards of conduct

nondescript   having no interesting features or qualities; undistinguished

nonentity a person of no interest or importance

nonpareil having no equal; peerless

nonplussed completely puzzled or bewildered

nonsectarian not associated with any religious denomination

non sequitur a statement that is unrelated to a previous one

nosh to snack

nostalgia sentimental longing for the past

nostrum a medicine or remedy of no real value

notable worthy of notice; outstanding

notary public a person legally authorized to witness and authenticate a signature on a document

noteworthy deserving notice; significant

notion a vague idea or belief; an impulse or whim

notorious widely and unfavorably known

notwithstanding in spite of; nevertheless

nourish to promote the growth or development of; to keep alive in the mind

nouveau riche a person who is newly rich

novel strikingly new or different

novice a person who is inexperienced in a job or situation

noxious harmful to the health; poisonous

nuance a subtle detail or quality; a slight difference or variation

nubile (of a woman) young and sexually attractive

nugatory worthless or futile

null legally invalid

nullify to make legally invalid; cancel

nullity nothingness; invalidity

numinous spiritual or supernatural; mysterious

nuptial relating to marriage or the wedding ceremony

nurture to nourish or cultivate

nutrient   any of the substances in food that
nourish the body, such as vitamins

nymphomania   abnormally high sexual
desire in a female

=O=

obdurate stubbornly resistant to persuasion or influence

obeisance obedience and respect

obelisk a tall stone column having four sloping sides and a pointed top

obese extremely fat

obfuscate to make unclear; confuse

obituary a notice in the newspaper of a person's death, often with a brief biography

objective (n) a goal or purpose

objective (adj) not influenced by emotions or personal beliefs; impartial

oblation an offering made to a deity

obligatory required or compulsory, as by law

oblique indirect; unclear

obliterate to remove all signs of; destroy

oblivion the state of being completely forgotten

oblivious totally unaware

oblong an object or shape that is longer than it is wide, esp. a rectangle

obloquy censure or blame; discredit or disgrace

obscene offensively sexual; indecent

obscure (v) to block from view; to make unclear

obscure (adj) difficult to understand or see

obsequious overly eager to please

obsession a persistent idea or desire that dominates the mind

obsolescence the process of becoming no longer useful or fashionable

obsolete no longer used

obstacle something that blocks progress or prevents success

obstetrics the branch of medicine that deals with pregnancy and childbirth

obstinate refusing to cooperate; stubborn

obstreperous noisy and difficult to control

obstruct to prevent from happening or being seen

obtrusive annoyingly noticeable

obtuse slow to understand; dull

obverse the other side; (of a coin) the front side

obviate to make unnecessary

Occident the countries of Europe and America

occlude to close, shut off, or block

occult relating to magical or supernatural powers

odalisque a female slave or concubine in a harem

oddity a person or thing that is unusual or not typical of its kind

ode a long, formal poem

odious deserving or causing hatred; detestable

odium intense hatred or disapproval

odometer a device that measures the distance that a vehicle has traveled

odoriferous or **odorous** having an odor; morally offensive

odyssey a long, adventurous journey

oedipal relating to sexual feelings for a parent of the opposite sex

oeuvre (OOV.ruh) the complete works of a writer or artist

offal the waste parts of a butchered animal

offensive causing displeasure or resentment

offices something done for another

officious self-important; bossy

ogle to look at with obvious sexual interest

ogre an ugly, cruel person

oleaginous oily

olfactory relating to the sense of smell

oligarchy   a form of government in which power is held by a few people

ombudsman   a person who investigates and resolves complaints, as from consumers

ominous   a sign of trouble or harm

omit   to leave out

omnipotent   all-powerful

omnipresent   present everywhere

omniscient   knowing all

omnivorous   eating both animal and plant foods

onanism   masturbation

oncology   the branch of medicine that deals with the diagnosis and treatment of cancerous tumors

onerous   burdensome; oppressive

onomatopoeia   the formation and use of a word that imitates the sound associated with it

onslaught   a violent attack or charge

ontogeny   the developmental history of an individual organism

ontology   a branch of study that deals with the nature of existence

onus   responsibility; burden

opalescent   having the shining or glowing colors of an opal

opaque   not letting light pass through; difficult to understand

operative (adj)   in effect; working correctly

operative (n)   a secret agent; spy

operetta   a short, comic opera

opiate   a sedative or narcotic

opine   to express an opinion

opportune   occurring at an advantageous time; useful for a particular purpose

opportunist   a person who takes advantage of every chance for self-advancement regardless of principles

oppress   to govern or control in an unfair

and harsh way; to worry or burden

oppressive   difficult to endure; harsh and unjust

opprobrium   disgrace caused by shameful conduct

optimal   most favorable

optimism   a tendency to be hopeful and to expect the most favorable outcome

optimize   to make as effective or useful as possible; to make the best of

option   freedom to choose; a choice or alternative; the right to buy or sell something at a set price

optional   not required; voluntary

opulence   great wealth and luxury

opus   an artistic work, such as a musical composition

oracle   a wise person who is a source of authoritative advice

oration   a formal public speech

oratorio   a large, formal musical work, usually on a religious theme

oratory   the art of skillful public speaking

orbit   the curved path followed by a planet, satellite, or spaceship around a celestial body

orchestrate   to arrange or organize carefully so as to achieve a desired result

ordain   to order by authority or law

ordinance   a regulation or law, esp. one enacted by a city government

ordnance   military supplies, including weapons and ammunition

ordure   manure; excrement

organism   a single living thing, such as a plant, animal or bacterium

orgasm   the moment of greatest excitement in sexual activity

Orient   the countries of Asia, esp. East Asia, including China and Japan

orient   to make familiar with a new situation or location

orientation the general direction of a person's choices in religion, politics, and sexuality

orifice an opening, as into a body cavity

originate to bring or come into existence

orisons prayers

ornate having a great many decorations

ornery mean and stubborn

orotund (of the voice) full and clear; (of speech or writing) too serious and important-sounding

orthodox following generally accepted or traditional beliefs

Orwellian characteristic of a totalitarian future world, as in the novels of George Orwell

oscillate to swing back and forth; to be undecided

osculation the act of kissing

osmosis a gradual absorption, as in learning by observation rather than formal study

ossify to form into bone; to become rigid and conventional

ostensible seeming to be; not actually true

ostentatious marked by a showy display of wealth

ostracize to refuse to include in a group

otiose idle; useless

oust to eject or remove

outrageous offensive; shocking

outset the beginning or start

outspoken frank and unreserved in speech

ovation an enthusiastic display of approval marked by loud applause

overbearing arrogant and domineering

overt not hidden; open; obvious

overthrow to remove from a position of power by force

overweening excessively conceited or overconfident

outflank to outmaneuver

outré (oo.TRAY) strange and shocking; unconventional

outtake a segment of film or tape that has been edited out

overarching including or overshadowing all other areas

overblown overdone or excessive; pretentious

overdraft an amount of money drawn from an account that exceeds the balance

overlay to cover one thing with another

overreach to fail by trying to achieve more than one is able to do

override to be more important than; to prevail over

overt not hidden; open; obvious

overtone something that is suggested but not clearly stated

overture an introductory piece of music; an initial offer or proposal in a negotiation

overweening excessively conceited or overconfident

overwrought very upset or nervous

ovulate to produce an egg cell

oxidize to combine chemically with oxygen, as when metal rusts

oxymoron a figure of speech that combines contradictory words

ozone a form of oxygen that is a poisonous gas in the lower atmosphere but in the upper atmosphere prevents ultraviolet rays from reaching the earth's surface

=P=

pachyderm any large, thick-skinned, hoofed mammal, such as the elephant

pacifism opposition to the use of violence to settle conflicts

pacify to calm or soothe; to make peaceable

paean a song of praise or thanksgiving

pagan a person who has no religious beliefs

palatable satisfactory to the taste; acceptable to the mind

palate the roof of the mouth; the sense of taste

palatial like a palace in size and grandeur

palaver idle talk; a conference or discussion

palette the range of colors typical of a particular artist

palimpsest a parchment used again after earlier writing has been erased; something that has many layers beneath the surface

palindrome a word or line that reads the same backward as forward

pall an atmosphere of gloom

pallet a small, narrow bed or a straw-filled mattress; a wooden platform used to transport heavy items

palliative a drug or treatment that relieves pain but does not cure; something that makes a problem seem less serious but does not solve it

pallid pale; dull

pallor unhealthy paleness

palpable easily noticed; obvious

palpate to examine by touch

palpitate to beat rapidly

paltry worthless; unimportant

panacea a cure for all ills or problems

panache great style; flair

pandemic (of a disease) spreading quickly throughout a very wide area

pandemonium wild confusion and panic

pander to cater to or exploit the weaknesses or vices of others

panegyric formal or elaborate praise

panjandrum a powerful or self-important official

panoply a wide range or collection of different things

panorama a full view or complete picture

pantheism belief in many or all gods; a belief that God lives in nature

pantheon a group of the most famous or admired persons in a particular activity or movement

pantomime a form of acting that consists of gestures without words

papier-mâché (PAY.per.ma.SHAY) a material made from wet paper mixed with glue which becomes hard when dry

papyrus a type of paper made from a tall water plant, esp. in ancient Egypt

par the usual standard or condition; equality in value

parable a short, simple story that teaches a moral or religious lesson

paradigm an example that serves as a model or pattern

paradox a situation or statement that seems to be contradictory but is possibly true; a person or thing that seems impossible to explain

paragon a model of excellence or perfection

paralegal a specially trained assistant to a lawyer

parallel a comparison showing close resemblance

parameter a fixed limit or boundary

paramount of greatest importance; primary; supreme

paramour a lover, esp. the illicit lover of a married person

paranoia an irrational feeling of fear and distrust of other people

parapet a low wall along the edge of a balcony, roof, or bridge

paraphernalia a collection of small objects, esp. equipment used for a particular activity

paraphrase to restate something in different words, esp. to make the meaning clearer

parentage descent from parents; origin

parenthetical (of a remark) said in addition to the main topic

par excellence being an example of excellence

pariah a person who is shunned by society; an outcast

parish the local area served by a church, or the members of the church

parity equality, as in status or value

parlance a special manner of speaking used by a particular group

parlay to use assets to greater advantage or profit

parley a discussion or conference

parliament the group of persons who make the laws of a country

parlous perilous; dangerous

parochial limited in range or interests; narrow

parody a comic imitation, as of a literary work, that ridicules the original; a poor imitation

paroxysm a sudden, violent outburst, as of emotion

parricide the killing of a parent, or one who commits this crime

parry to avoid skillfully

parse to analyze a sentence in terms of its parts of speech

parsimonious stingy; frugal

partake to take part; to share or participate

partiality a favorable bias

partisan a strong supporter, as of a cause

partition to divide into areas

parturition childbirth

parvenu a person who has suddenly acquired wealth or success but not social acceptance

pas de deux (pah de DUH) a dance for two performers

pasha a former title of high officials in countries under Turkish rule

passé no longer in fashion; out-of-date

passel an undetermined number of things

pastiche a literary, musical, or artistic piece that consists of parts taken from other sources

pastoral relating to quiet country life

patent (n) an exclusive right to make and sell an invention

patent (adj) clear; obvious

paterfamilias the male head of a household; father

paternal of or from a father; related through a father

paternity the fact of being a father

pathetic causing feelings of pity or compassion; causing feelings of contempt or disdain

pathogen something that causes disease, such as a virus

pathology the scientific study of disease

pathos a quality in life or art that brings out feelings of sympathy or sorrow

patina a thin surface layer that develops on something as a result of age, esp. the green oxidation on ancient bronzes and coins

patois   a local or regional dialect

patriarch   the father and leader of a family or tribe

patrician   a person of high social rank; an aristocrat

patricide   killing one's father

patrimony   money or property inherited from one's father or ancestors

patronage   the business that comes from customers; the power of public officials to grant favors to their supporters

patronize   to be a customer of; to behave in an offensively superior manner toward

patter   smooth rapid speech; fast talk

paucity   short supply; scarcity

pauper   a very poor person

Pavlovian   relating to a conditioned or predictable reaction

pawn   a person who is used to further the purposes of another

peccadillo   a minor sin or offense

peckish   (British) somewhat hungry

pecuniary   relating to money

pedagogue   an educator; a difficult and demanding teacher

pedantic   overly concerned with book learning and formal rules

pederasty   sexual relations between a man and a boy

pedestrian   showing little imagination; commonplace; ordinary

pedigree   an ancestral line, esp. of a purebred animal; distinguished ancestry

pedophile   an adult who is sexually interested in children

peer   a person who has equal standing with others, as in age or rank

peerless   without equal; unmatched

peevish   irritable; annoyed

pejorative   expressing a critical or negative judgment

pell-mell   in a hurried and confused

manner

pellucid clear in meaning or expression

pelt (n) the fur and skin of an animal

pelt (v) to attack by throwing things

penal relating to punishment

penance the act of atoning for one's sins or wrongdoing

penchant a strong liking or tendency

pendant a hanging ornament, as on a necklace

pendulous hanging loosely

penitent feeling sorrow and regret for wrongdoing; repentant

penitentiary a prison

pensive in deep and serious thought

penultimate next to last

penumbra a shadowy or indefinite area

penurious extremely stingy; very poor

peon a person who does low-level, unskilled work

per annum by the year; annually

per capita by or for each person

perceive to become aware of through the senses; to understand

perceptive showing keen insight and understanding

percipient characterized by ease and quickness in perceiving

percussion the group of musical instruments that are struck to produce a sound, such as a drum or piano

per diem by the day; daily

perdition a state of damnation; hell

peregrination a long journey, esp. on foot

peremptory not to be denied or refused, as a command; arrogant and dictatorial

perennial lasting indefinitely; repeated regularly

perfervid extremely ardent; impassioned

perfidious treacherous; deceitful

perforce necessary by force of circumstances

perfunctory done as a routine duty without care or interest

peril grave risk; something that may cause injury or destruction

perilous hazardous; dangerous

perimeter the outer edge of a figure or area

peripatetic walking or traveling about

peripheral located on the outer edge; not of central importance

periphery the boundary of a surface or area; the outskirts of a city

perjury (in law) the act of giving false testimony under oath

perk a special benefit; perquisite

permeable capable of being passed through

permeate to flow into and spread throughout

permissible allowable

permissive allowing too much freedom; indulgent

permutation any of the various ways in which a set of things can be ordered

pernicious causing great harm or injury

peroration a long speech, or the concluding part that sums it up

perpendicular meeting a given line at right angles; vertical or upright

perpetrate to commit a crime

perpetuate to cause to continue indefinitely; to cause to be remembered

perpetuity endless duration or existence

perplexed puzzled or confused

perquisite a special benefit or privilege received in addition to regular income

persecute to treat unjustly or cruelly; oppress

persevere to continue to pursue a goal in spite of opposition or difficulty

persiflage light, bantering talk

personable having a pleasing personality;

likable and attractive

persona non grata unacceptable or unwelcome

personify to represent ideas or objects in human form; to be a perfect example of

perspective mental outlook

perspicacious quick in noticing or understanding things accurately

perspicuous clearly expressed or presented

persuasive having the power to persuade

pert stylish and saucy

pertain to belong or relate to

pertinacious holding firmly to a purpose or opinion

pertinent directly related or relevant

perturb to disturb someone's peace of mind; to upset

peruse to read or examine carefully

pervade to spread throughout

pervasive present or noticeable throughout

perverse stubbornly opposing what is right or reasonable; wicked or corrupt

perversion sexual behavior that is considered abnormal or deviant

pessimism a tendency to stress the negative or anticipate the worst outcome

pestilence a deadly epidemic disease

petard an explosive device

petite small and dainty

petrify to turn to stone; to paralyze with terror

pettifogger one who quibbles over trifles; an underhanded and unethical lawyer

petulant ill-tempered; irritable

phalanx a body of troops in close formation; a group of people united for a common purpose

phallic related to or shaped like the penis

phallus the penis

phantasm a creation of the imagination; something that is seen but is not there

phantasmagoria a shifting series of

illusions, as in a dream

phantom a ghostly illusion

phenomenon (pl. **phenomena**) something unusual that attracts interest; a remarkable person or event

philanderer a man who has affairs with many women

philanthropist a person who donates money and time to promote good causes

philistine a person who is indifferent to the fine arts and culture

Phillipic bitter denunciation in speech or writing

philology the study of language, esp. its history and development

philosophy the study of the truths and principles of life and morals; a particular belief or viewpoint

phlegm a thick mucus produced by the respiratory tract

phlegmatic having a calm or unemotional temperament

phoenix a symbol of immortality or rebirth

phoneme the smallest unit of sound that can distinguish one word from another

phonetics the study of the sounds of speech

phraseology a manner or style of verbal expression

phrenetic wildly excited; frenzied

physic a laxative

physiognomy the physical appearance of the face

picaresque involving the adventures of a clever rogue, as in a type of fiction originating in Spain

picayune of little value or importance

piebald (of a horse) having patches of two colors, esp. black and white

pièce de résistance the most important or best thing in a set or series

pied-à-terre (pee.ay.de.TARE) an

apartment for part-time use

piffling   of little worth; trifling

pilfer   to steal a small amount

pilgrimage   a long journey to a special place

pillage   to strip ruthlessly of property by violence, as in war

pillory   to expose to public ridicule or abuse

pinion   to fasten a person's arms so they cannot move

pinnacle   a peak or summit

pious   showing religious reverence; pretending to have sincere feelings or religious motives

piquant   interesting and exciting

pique   to annoy or irritate; to arouse or stimulate

pirouette   (in ballet) a full turn on the toes or ball of the foot

pissant   a worthless person

piteous   arousing pity or sympathy

pith   the central or essential part

pithy   brief, forceful, and meaningful

pitiable   arousing or deserving pity

pitiless   having no pity; merciless

pittance   a very small wage

pivotal   of critical importance

pixilated   slightly eccentric or unbalanced; whimsical

placate   to calm someone's anger, as by agreeing to demands

placebo   a substance that looks like a medicine but has no real effect, given to please a patient or as a control in tests on actual drugs

placid   calm; peaceful

plagiarism   the act of using another's writings and ideas as one's own

plaintiff   the person or group that files a lawsuit in court

plaintive   expressing sorrow or distress

plangent having a loud and sorrowful sound, as a bell

platitude a boring and obvious saying that is often repeated

platonic referring to a relationship that is affectionate but not sexual

plaudits praise

plausible seemingly true or logical

plebeian common; ordinary; crude

plebiscite a direct vote by all the voters of a country or district in regard to a proposal

plenary attended by all the qualified members of an organization

plenipotentiary a diplomatic agent having full power to transact business

plenitude fullness or abundance

plethora overabundance; excess

pliable (of a substance) easily shaped or bent; (of a person) easily influenced or controlled

pliant pliable; adaptable

ploy a trick to gain advantage

pluck courage and spirit

plumb (n) a weight hung from the end of a cord and used to measure the depth of water or to determine if something is vertical

plumb (v) to measure depth; to examine closely

plunder to take large amounts of property by force

pluralism the existence of different minority groups within a society

plurality (in an election) the largest number of votes among the candidates

plutocrat a person whose wealth gives him power and influence

ply to work at a trade; to travel over a route; to keep supplying someone with food, drink, or questions

pneumatic filled with compressed air

poach to cook gently in a hot liquid; to hunt or fish illegally on private property

poetaster an inferior poet

poetic justice a particularly appropriate punishment or reward

pogrom organized persecution and killing, esp. of Jews

poignant deeply moving

pol a politician

polarize to divide into sharply opposing factions

polemic a controversial argument, esp. an attack on a specific belief

polis an ancient Greek city-state

politesse courteous formality; politeness

politic showing good judgment; tactful; diplomatic

polity a particular form or system of government

poltroon a wretched coward

polyandry the practice of having more than one husband at one time

polychrome being of various colors

polygamy the practice of having more than one wife or husband at one time

polyglot a person who speaks many languages

polygyny the practice of having more than one wife at one time

polymath a person of great learning in several fields of study

polymorphous having or passing through many forms or stages

polysyllabic having more than three syllables

polytheism belief in more than one god

pomp showy display or ceremony

pompous marked by a showy display of self-importance

ponderous slow-moving and dull

pontiff a Roman Catholic pope or priest

pontificate to speak in a dogmatic or

163

pompous manner

popinjay   a vain, shallow person

populate   to supply with inhabitants

populism   representation of the views and interests of the common people

porcine   pertaining to or resembling swine

portal   a large, impressive gate or entrance

portend   to serve as an advance indication, as of future danger

portent   a warning about the future

portmanteau   combining a wide range of items or features

poseur   a person who assumes a character or manner in order to impress others

posit   to assume as a fact or principle

posterior   the buttocks; the back end of something

posterity   future generations

posthumous   occurring after one's death

postmortem   an examination of a body to determine cause of death; an analysis of a failure

postprandial   after a meal

postscript   an addition at the end of a letter or document

postulant   a person who applies for something, as for admission into a religious order

postulate   to assume the existence or truth of something without proof

posture   the way the body is held; a policy or attitude of an organization or government

potable   fit to drink

potboiler   a literary work of low quality that is produced quickly for financial gain

potentate   a powerful ruler

potential   possible

potentiate   to increase the effectiveness of; intensify

potpourri   a fragrant mixture of dried flowers and herbs, or other things

poultice a soft heated mass spread on cloth and applied to a sore or an inflamed area

practicable capable of being done

pragmatic using common sense to solve problems

pragmatism a philosophy of dealing with problems that emphasizes practical results rather than theories

pratfall a humiliating blunder

prate to talk excessively and foolishly

preamble a formal introduction to a document that explains its purpose

precarious not secure or safe; shaky

precede to come before or exist earlier

precedent an example for similar actions or circumstances in the future

precept a rule to use for action

precinct a local police station; a designated area covered by police authority

precincts an area or enclosure with definite boundaries

precipice a steep cliff; the edge of danger

precipitate to cause to happen suddenly

precipitous extremely steep; declining fast

précis (PRAY.see) a concise summary

preclude to make impossible; prevent

precocious (of a child) advanced in mental skills or abilities

precognition knowledge of a future event through extrasensory means

preconceive to form an opinion too early, esp. without enough knowledge

precursor something that comes before another thing, esp. if it influences or leads to it

predatory preying upon others, as for food or personal gain

predestined determined in advance, as by fate

predicate to base an action or belief on something else

165

predilection a liking or tendency

predispose to influence beforehand; to make someone vulnerable, as to a disease

predominant being the most noticeable, important, or largest in number

predominate to overshadow others, as in importance

preeminent superior to all others; outstanding

preempt to take the place of

preen to pride oneself on an action or quality

prefabricate to make or build something beforehand

preface an introduction to a book or speech

prefatory introductory

prefect a person appointed to any of various positions of authority, as in ancient Rome

prefigure to show or represent beforehand; foreshadow

prefix a letter or group of letters placed at the beginning of a word to make a new word

prehensile adapted for seizing or grasping, as the tail of an animal

prelate a church official of high rank, as a bishop

prelude a preceding event or performance that introduces what follows

premeditate to plan or plot in advance, esp. a crime

premier first in status or importance; foremost

premiere the first public performance, as of a play or film

premise a basis for a line of reasoning

premises property and the buildings on it

premonition a feeling that something bad will happen

preponderance superiority in weight,

amount, or importance

prepossessing interesting, noticeable, or attractive

preposterous totally absurd

preprandial before dinner

prepubescent referring to the period of development before sexual maturity

prequel a sequel to a film, book, or play that deals with earlier events than the original

prerequisite something required beforehand

prerogative a right or privilege

presage to indicate something in advance; foretell

prescient knowing or suggesting correctly what will happen in the future

presentiment a feeling that something bad is about to happen

preside to occupy the position of authority, as at a meeting

prestidigitation sleight of hand; magic

prestige respect and admiration arising from achievement or rank

presume to assume that something is true; to do something without permission; to take unfair advantage

presumptuous going beyond what is right or proper; taking advantage

presuppose to require as a necessary condition in advance

pretense a false show of something

pretentious acting in a showy or affected manner

preternatural more than is usual or natural; extraordinary

pretext a pretended reason for doing something

prevail to triumph; to be common or current

prevalent of wide extent or occurrence; in general use

prevaricate to speak falsely

preventative a drug or other substance which prevents disease

preventive serving to prevent or hinder

priapism continuous, abnormal erection of the penis

primacy the state of being first in order or importance

prima donna the principal female singer of an opera company; an irritable, haughty woman

prima facie based on what seems to be the truth at first sight

primal characteristic of the earliest time in the existence of a person or thing

primate a member of the highest order of mammals, including humans and apes

primer (PRIM.er) a book that covers the basics of a subject

primeval belonging to the earliest ages; ancient; prehistoric

primogenitor ancestor; forefather

primogeniture inheritance of all a family's property by the eldest son

primordial characteristic of the earliest beginnings, as of the universe; connected with an early stage of development

primp to groom oneself with excessive care

priority the right to precede others in order or rank; something given special attention

pristine remaining in a pure state; unspoiled

privation lack of the necessities of life

privy allowed to know something secret

prix fixe (pree FEEKS) a fixed price charged for a complete meal

proactive taking action in anticipation of a future problem

probate the official proving of a will as authentic

probation a trial period for testing a person's abilities or qualifications; the conditional release of a convicted criminal under supervision

probative affording proof or evidence

probity integrity and honesty

problematic posing a problem or question

pro bono done or donated without charge

proboscis the long, movable nose of some animals; (humorous) the human nose, esp. if large

proclivity a tendency

procrastinate to keep delaying something that must be done

procreate to produce offspring

procrustean producing conformity by arbitrary means

procurer a pimp

prodigal recklessly wasteful or extravagant

prodigious far beyond what is usual in extent or degree

prodigy a young person with extraordinary talent or ability

prodrome an early symptom that a disease is developing

profane unholy or irreligious; coarse or vulgar

profanity vulgar language

profess to declare openly

proffer to offer

proficient skillful; expert

profiteer to make excessive profits on the sale of goods in short supply

profligate recklessly wasteful; shamelessly immoral

pro forma done as a matter of form

profound emotionally or intellectually deep

profuse abundant; plentiful

profusion a great quantity or amount

progenitor a direct ancestor

progeny offspring; descendants

prognosis a prediction or forecast, esp. of the likely course or outcome of a disease

prognosticate to forecast from present indications

progression a series of related events

progressive moving steadily forward; favoring new ideas and social reform

prohibitive tending to discourage the use or purchase of something

prole a member of the working class

proletariat the working class

proliferate to grow or spread rapidly

prolific highly productive

prolix tediously long and wordy

prologue a preface or introductory part, as to a novel

prolong to lengthen in duration

promenade a stroll or walk in a public place

prominent standing out and easily seen; well-known and respected

promiscuous having numerous sexual partners

promissory (of a note) agreeing to repay a loan

promontory a narrow area of high land that projects into the sea

promulgate to set forth or teach publicly, as beliefs or ideas

prone lying with the face down; tending or inclined

propaganda information or ideas spread, as by a government, with the intention of influencing people's opinions

propagate to cause to multiply from the parent stock, as a plant; to spread, as beliefs

propensity a natural tendency or inclination

prophetic predicting the future

prophylactic a device used to prevent

conception or venereal disease, esp. a condom; a device or process used to promote cleanliness or prevent disease

prophylaxis prevention of the spread of disease

propinquity nearness in time or place

propitiate to please and calm; appease

propitious likely to succeed; favorable

proponent a person who speaks in support of something; an advocate

propose to put forward for consideration; suggest

propound to offer for consideration or acceptance

proprietary relating to an owner or ownership

propriety the quality of being proper or suitable; conformity to established standards of conduct

propulsion a force that pushes something forward

pro rata according to a certain rate; in proportion

prorate to divide or distribute in proportion

prosaic lacking interest or imagination; boring

proscenium the part of a theater stage in front of the curtain

proscribe to prohibit; forbid

prose the ordinary form of written or spoken language, as opposed to poetry

proselytize to attempt to change someone's religious beliefs or opinions

prosody a particular system of poetic meter and versification

prospective likely or expected

prospectus a printed description of the major features of a proposed commercial venture

prostate referring to a gland that surrounds the urethra in males

prosthesis   an artificial body part, such as a limb, that substitutes for a missing or defective part

prostrate   lying face down, as in submission; physically or emotionally exhausted

protagonist   the main character in a play or novel

protean   easily and continually changing; variable

protégé   a person who is taught and protected by a more experienced person

protestation   a strong declaration

protocol   a set of rules governing proper conduct in particular circumstances

prototype   an original example of something from which all later forms are developed

protract   to extend in time; lengthen

protrude   to stick out

protuberant   bulging or swelling outward

provenance   place or source of origin

provender   food; provisions

proverbial   widely known; commonly accepted as true

providence   divine control and protection

providential   happening at the right time; fortunate

province   a political division of a country; a person's area of interest or responsibility

provincial   having narrow views or interests; unsophisticated

proviso   a specified condition or demand, as in an agreement

provocateur   a person who causes trouble or dissension; an agitator

provocation   a reason to protest or fight; an insult

provocative   provoking discussion or anger; sexually suggestive

provoke   to make angry; to stir up or incite a response

provost a high-ranking university administrator

proximate very near; close

proximity nearness in place, time, or relation

proxy authorization to act for another person

prudent sensible in practical matters

prurient having or causing lustful or indecent thoughts

pseudo false

pseudonym a fictitious name used by an author; pen name

psyche the human mind or spirit

psychedelic relating to or producing distorted sensory perceptions or altered states of awareness

psychic relating to or having knowledge or mental abilities beyond the natural range of perception

psychopath a person having an aggressively antisocial mental illness

psychosis a mental disorder in which there is loss of contact with reality

psychosomatic relating to physical disorders that are caused by emotional factors

pubescent having reached sexual maturity

pubic relating to the area around the external sex organs in humans

publicity information released to the public to generate interest

puckish mischievous

puerile childish; foolish

pugilist a person who fights with the fists professionally; a boxer

pugnacious inclined to quarrel or fight easily; combative

puissance power; might

pulchritude physical beauty

pulmonary relating to the lungs

pummel to beat rapidly with the fists

punctilious strictly observant of the formalities of conduct

punctual acting or arriving exactly on time

punctuate to interrupt at intervals

pundit an expert or authority

pungent sharp; biting; having a strong odor

punitive inflicting punishment

purblind nearly blind; lacking in understanding or imagination

purchase a firm grip or grasp on something

purgative a laxative

purgatory a condition or place of temporary punishment or suffering

purge to eliminate undesirable members from a government or political party; to take a strong laxative

purist a person who strictly observes traditional correctness

puritanical very strict in moral or religious matters

purlieu neighborhood; environs

purloin to steal

purport (n) general meaning; significance

purport (v) to deliberately give a false impression

pursuant in accordance with

purulent containing or discharging pus

purvey to supply provisions, esp. as a business

purview the limit of a person's responsibility or interest

pusillanimous cowardly and weak

putative commonly regarded as such

putrefy to decay with a foul odor; rot

putrid in a state of foul decay; utterly worthless; rotten

putsch a sudden and secretly planned attempt to overthrow a government

pygmy   an individual of unusually small
   size; a person of little importance or skill
pyre   a pile of wood for burning a dead
   body
pyromania   a compulsion to set fires
pyrotechnics   a display of fireworks
pyrrhic   (of a victory) achieved at too great
   a cost

=Q=

quadrennial occurring every four years

quadriplegic a person who has paralysis of the entire body below the neck

quadroon a person with one-quarter black ancestry

quadruped a four-footed animal

quaff to drink heartily

quagmire a very difficult and complicated situation

quail to feel or show fear

quaint pleasantly unusual or old-fashioned

qualitative relating to the quality of a situation rather than to measurable facts

qualm an uneasy feeling or doubt

quandary a state of uncertainty about what to do

quantify to determine or describe the amount of something

quantitative relating to quantity or number

quantum (in physics) the smallest amount or unit of energy

quantum leap a sudden great change or advance, as in knowledge

quarantine a period of enforced isolation of an infected person or animal intended to keep a disease from spreading

quarry (n) something that is hunted

quarry (v) to cut stone from a mining pit

quash to stop firmly; put down or suppress

quasi almost, but not completely; resembling

quaver to tremble

quay (KEY) a landing place for ships; wharf

queasy nauseated; squeamish

quell to put down by force, as a revolt; to calm, as fears

quench to put out or extinguish

querulous full of complaints

query a question; to express doubts about

quest a long search for something difficult to find

queue a line of people waiting their turn

quibble to argue over minor details

quiddity the essential nature of something; a trifling point or quibble

quid pro quo something given or taken in return for something else

quiescent motionless; still

quietude stillness; tranquility

quintessence the purest essence or concentration of something

quintessential being a perfect example of a type

quintuple to multiply by five

quip a short, witty remark

quirk an unusual habit or mannerism; an unpredictable event

quisling a traitor to one's country

quixotic visionary and impractical

quizzical puzzled; questioning

quorum the minimum number of members of a group that must be present to transact business

quota a fixed amount or number that is officially allowed or required

quotidian daily

quotient the result of dividing one number by another; quota or share

=R=

rabbi a teacher and spiritual leader in the Jewish religion

rabid overzealous; fanatical

raconteur a person who tells amusing or interesting stories

raffish carelessly unconventional

raft a large quantity of something

rail to utter bitter complaints or criticism

railroad to convict a person quickly without sufficient evidence; to push a bill hastily through a legislature

raiment clothes

raison d'être (ray.zon DET.ruh) reason for existence

rakish bold in style or action

rambunctious noisy and out of control

ramification a result or consequence of an action

rampant widespread and uncontrollable

rampart a large barrier built around a fort to protect it

ramrod to accomplish by force

rancor deep and bitter hatred

randy full of sexual desire

rankle to cause continuing annoyance or resentment

ransack to search through vigorously, esp. in order to steal

rant to speak loudly in an uncontrolled or angry way

rapacious extremely greedy or grasping

rapine violent seizure of another's property

rappel to go down a steep slope by means of a rope that is secured above

rapprochement an establishment of harmonious relations between opposing groups

rapscallion a rascal or rogue

rapt deeply absorbed; enraptured

raptor a bird of prey

rapture great joy or pleasure; ecstasy

rarefied lofty or elevated

rash too bold or hasty

ratchet to move up or down by degrees

ratify to approve and make official

ratiocination logical reasoning

rational able to think clearly; based on logical thought

rationale the basic reasons for a particular set of thoughts or actions

rationalize to give seemingly reasonable explanations for one's behavior

raucous loud and harsh; disorderly

ravage to damage severely

ravenous extremely hungry; voracious

ravish to seize and take by force

ravishing extremely beautiful; dazzling

raze to tear down or destroy

reactionary a person who is opposed to political or social change; a conservative

readily willingly; easily

realist a person who expects only what seems possible and tends to view things as they really are

realistic (of a person) practical; (of paintings, books, etc.) accurately depicted

realm an area of knowledge; a kingdom

realpolitik practical politics based on power rather than ideals

rebuff a quick and complete rejection

rebuke to criticize sharply

rebut to prove something false or wrong, as by evidence

recalcitrant unwilling to obey orders or be controlled

recant to withdraw formally a statement or belief previously held

recapitulate to repeat in shorter form; summarize

receptive willing to consider suggestions or offers

recession a time of weak economic activity

recessive (of a gene) appearing in offspring only if supplied by both parents

recherché (re.share.SHAY) very rare or choice; excessively refined or affected

recidivism repeated relapse into criminal behavior

recipient a person who receives something

reciprocal given or owed to each other

reciprocate to give something equal in exchange

reciprocity mutual exchange

recital a performance of music or dance by a solo artist

reckoning an accounting, as for things done or received

recluse a person who lives alone and apart from society

recognizance a legal obligation requiring appearance in court under penalty of a forfeiture of money

recollect to remember

recompense to make payment to, as for loss or damage

reconcile to bring persons into harmony or agreement; to bring oneself to accept something unwanted

recondite very profound or difficult to understand

reconnaissance an exploration of an area, esp. to gather military information

reconnoiter to survey an enemy position for military purposes

reconstitute to return a dried substance to its original state by adding water

recount to tell in detail

recoup to gain back, as money lost

recourse access to a person or thing for help or protection

recrimination argument between people

who are accusing each other

recrudesce to break out or become active again

rectify to set right; correct

rectitude strict honesty and morality

recumbent lying down; reclining

recurrent happening repeatedly

recuse to disqualify oneself as judge in a particular case because of a conflict of interest

redact to put into proper literary form; edit

redeem see redemption

redemption rescue, salvation, atonement; recovery of payment

red herring a misleading clue that diverts attention from the matter at hand

redolent smelling strongly of something

redoubt a defended position or protective barrier

redoubtable commanding respect; formidable

redound to have a good or bad effect; to reflect upon a person

redress to remedy a wrong

reductio ad absurdum the carrying of something to an absurd conclusion

reductionism oversimplification

redundant more than is needed; something repeated

refraction the bending of light waves, as through a prism

refractory stubbornly disobedient

refrain (n) lines repeated several times in a song or poem

refrain (v) to stop oneself from doing something

refulgent shining brightly

refurbish to make something look new again

refute to prove something to be incorrect

regale to entertain or amuse

regalia   special clothes and decorations worn on ceremonial occasions

regatta   a boat race

regime   a government; a system of care or treatment

regimen   a way of living or eating

regimented   managed in a rigidly uniform or disciplined manner

regnant   (as a monarch) reigning

regress   to revert to a previous condition

regurgitate   to vomit

rehabilitate   to restore to good condition

reign   (n)   the period during which a monarch is in power

reign   (v)   to rule as a monarch; to be widely felt

reimburse   to pay back

rein   to hold back

reincarnation   rebirth in a new person or form after death

reinstate   to restore to a previous position

reiterate   to repeat

rejoinder   an answer in response to another's answer

rejuvenate   to make young or vigorous again

rekindle   to make something burn again, as fire or passion

relapse   to fall back again into an earlier condition

relativism   a theory that holds that moral values are not absolute but may vary with individuals and their environment

relativity   either of two theories developed by Albert Einstein dealing with the relationship between space, time, and energy

relegate   to move something to a less important rank or position

relent   to soften in feeling or determination; to become less severe

relentless   continuing in a severe or

determined way; unyielding

relevant   related to the matter at hand; pertinent

relic   an object or tradition surviving from the past

relinquish   to give up or hand over

relish   to enjoy greatly

reluctant   unwilling

remand   to send an accused person back to custody to await trial

remedial   designed to improve or correct

reminiscence   the act of recalling the past, esp. pleasant memories

remiss   careless about duty; neglectful

remission   a period of time when an illness is less severe or disappears entirely

remittance   money sent in payment

remnant   a surviving trace; a leftover piece of cloth

remonstrate   to plead in protest or complaint

remorse   deep regret for wrongdoing

remuneration   payment for services or losses

renaissance   a rebirth or revival, as of a style of art

renascent   being reborn or made new again

rend   to pull apart violently

render   to cause to become; to provide, as assistance

rendezvous   a prearranged meeting, esp. a secret one

rendition   an interpretation, as of a piece of music

renegade   an outlaw

renege   to fail to keep a promise or agreement

renounce   to give up a title formally; to quit

renovate   to restore or renew, as a house

renown   widespread fame

renunciation   a giving up or rejection

reparable   able to be repaired or remedied

reparation   compensation for wrongdoing

repartee   quick, witty remarks in conversation

repast   a meal

repatriate   to send a person back to his or her country

repellent (n)   a substance used to drive away pests

repellent (adj)   causing disgust

repent   to feel guilt and regret for one's actions

repercussions   consequent reactions

repertoire   all the works that a person or company is prepared to perform

repertory   the repeated performance of several plays by one company of actors

repine   to fret or complain; to feel sad

replenish   to restore a supply of

replete   full of

replicate   to duplicate or reproduce

reportage   the technique of reporting the news

repose   the state of being at rest

repository   a place where things are kept safe

reprehensible   deserving blame; shameful

repress   to hold back, as memories; to put down by force

reprieve   a formal delay of impending punishment; a temporary relief, as of pain

reprimand   to scold or criticize angrily or officially

reprisal   retaliation against an enemy for injury or damage

reprise   (re.PREEZ)   to repeat, as part of a piece of music

reproach   criticism; blame

reprobate   a morally bad person

reprove   to criticize or correct

repudiate   to reject as untrue or

unreasonable

repugnant causing dislike or disgust

repulsive disgusting

reputable having a good reputation

reputedly said to be

requiem a religious service or piece of music to honor the dead

requiescat in pace (reck.ees.caht in PAH.che) rest in peace

requisite required; essential

requisition a formal written request for something needed

requite to repay in kind, as for a service or injury

rescind to make void; annul or repeal

rescission the act of annulling

reserved marked by self-restraint in words and actions

reservoir an extra supply

residential limited to places where people live rather than businesses

residual pertaining to something left over

residue something that remains after a part is removed or used

resigned accepting something as inevitable

resilient able to recover quickly from difficulty

resolute firm or determined

resolve firmness of purpose

resonant having a deep and clear tone

resort to turn to for help, or as a means of accomplishing something

respectful showing proper respect

respective relating individually to each of two or more persons

respectively each in the order named

respite a pause or rest from something difficult

resplendent dazzling in appearance

responsive ready to act or help; cooperative

restitution   repayment for loss or injury

restive   impatient or restless; difficult to control

résumé   a brief outline of one's work history and education

resurgence   a rising or coming back to life

resurrect   to bring back to life

resuscitate   to bring back to consciousness

retain   to keep possession of

retainer   a fee paid to secure professional services, as of a lawyer

retaliate   to pay back an injury in kind

retard   to slow the progress of

retentive   having the power to retain, as in the memory

reticent   unwilling to speak out; shy or reserved

retinue   a group of followers

retiring   quiet and shy

retort   a quick, sharp reply

retreat   the withdrawal of a military force; a private, quiet place

retrench   to cut back money or activity; to economize

retribution   something given or demanded in payment for a wrong

retrieve   to get back; recover

retroactive   effective as of a date that has already passed

retrofit   to furnish with new parts or equipment something previously manufactured or constructed

retrograde   having a backward motion or direction

retrogress   to move backward into a worse position or state

retrospect   contemplation of past time or events

retrospection   the process of looking back on the past

retrospective   an exhibit showing an artist's work over a period of years

revamp   to revise or redo

revanchism   a political policy aimed at regaining lost territory or status

revelation   something made known or disclosed

revelry   noisy celebration

reverberate   to continue to sound; to echo repeatedly

revere   to respect and honor

reverie   a pleasant, dreamlike state

revert   to return to a former condition or belief

revile   to speak of with contempt

revise   to alter or amend

revulsion   a strong feeling of disgust

rhapsodize   to express great enthusiasm for something

rhetoric   the art of using language effectively; elaborate or insincere language

rhetorical question   a question that is asked solely to make a statement and not to elicit a reply

rheumy   filled with mucus

rhinoplasty   plastic surgery of the nose

rhinovirus   any of a widespread group of viruses responsible for the common cold

ribald   vulgar or indecent

ricochet   to bounce off a surface and change direction, as a bullet

rictus   a gaping grin

rife   abundant; prevalent

riffraff   people regarded as worthless or undesirable

rift   a break in friendly relations

rigmarole   an elaborately complicated procedure

rigor   strictness or inflexibility; harshness of living conditions

rigor mortis   stiffening of the body after death

rigorous   precisely accurate; severe or

harsh

rile to anger or irritate

riparian legal rights to a natural supply of water; referring to the bank of a river

riposte a quick, sharp reply

risible laughable; ridiculous

risqué slightly indelicate or improper sexual reference

rite a ceremonial act

ritual a procedure or ceremony that is faithfully followed

riven split apart

riveting holding the eye or attention

rococo highly ornate or detailed in style

roister to act in a boisterous manner

rollicking carefree and high-spirited

roman à clef a novel in which the characters are based on real people

romanticize to treat in a romantic or idealized way

romp to frolic in a lively manner

Rorschach test a diagnostic test of personality and intellect based on interpretations of inkblots

roseate overly optimistic

Rosetta stone a stone slab found in 1799 that made possible the deciphering of Egyptian hieroglyphics

roster a list of names

rostrum a stage or platform for public speaking

rotate to turn around a fixed point; to take turns in sequence

rote learning by memory or habit rather than by understanding

rotogravure the magazine section of a newspaper

rotund rounded in shape; plump

rotunda a large circular hall surmounted by a dome

roué a man of low character

rounder a habitual drunkard

roundly   vigorously or unsparingly

rouse   to wake up

roust   to force out

roustabout   an unskilled laborer, as one who works on docks or in oil fields

rout   an overwhelming defeat

RSVP   please respond

Rubenesque   plump and voluptuous

rubric   a category or classification

ruddy   having a healthy, reddish color; the reddish fur of an animal

rudimentary   basic; elementary

rue   to feel sorrow or deep regret over

ruinous   causing great harm or destruction

ruminate   to think long and deeply about something

ruse   a trick or deception

rusticate   to spend time in the country

ruthless   showing no pity; cruel

=S=

sabbatical   a leave of absence given to college professors for research, study, or travel

sabotage   destructive action intended to hinder the plans of an enemy or competitor

saccharine   insincerely sweet; overly sentimental

sacerdotal   of priests; priestly

sack   to loot or plunder a captured city

sackcloth   a garment of coarse cloth worn to show repentance or grief

sacred cow   something considered to be exempt from criticism or opposition

sacrilege   violation of something held sacred

sacrosanct   regarded as being beyond criticism or change

sadism   sexual pleasure derived from inflicting pain on others

sadomasochism   sexual pleasure derived from inflicting or receiving pain

sagacious   showing wisdom and good judgment

sage   a very wise person

salacious   arousing or appealing to sexual desire; lustful

salient   most obvious or important

saline   relating to or containing salt

salivate   to produce saliva, as in anticipation of eating

salubrious   promoting good health

salutary   healthful; wholesome

salutation   a greeting, as at the opening of a letter

salve   to soothe or comfort

salvo   a round of gunfire; a verbal attack on an opponent

sanctimonious hypocritically religious or virtuous

sanction to give formal approval or official permission to; (in law) a penalty for unlawful behavior

sanctity holiness or sacredness

sanctuary a safe, protected place; asylum

sanctum a private place or retreat

sang-froid coolness of mind in a difficult situation; composure

sanguinary bloody; bloodthirsty

sanguine optimistic; cheerful

sans souci (French) carefree

sapient showing wisdom and sound judgment

sarcophagus a stone coffin, usually displayed as a monument

sardonic mockingly scornful

sartorial relating to clothes or style of dress

satanic relating to the Devil; extremely cruel or evil

sate to satisfy fully an appetite or desire

satiate to satisfy to the full; sate

satirize to attack or criticize by means of ridicule

satori sudden enlightenment in Zen Buddhism

satrap a subordinate official

saturnine gloomy and unfriendly

satyr a lecherous man

saucy impertinent; disrespectful

savant a person of great learning

savior a person who saves another

savoir-faire the ability to do or say the right thing in any situation

savor to taste and enjoy

sawbuck a ten dollar bill

sayonara (Japanese) good-bye

scab a worker hired to replace striking union workers

scabrous indecent; obscene

scalawag a rascal

scandal a public disgrace

scandalous disgraceful; shocking

scant barely sufficient

scapegoat a person or group that is made to bear the blame for others

scarce not easy to find or obtain

scarify to hurt with severe criticism

scathing harshly critical

scatological preoccupied with obscenity and excrement

scavenge to search for something useful in discarded material

scenario a description of possible future actions or events; the script for a movie

scepter a decorated rod carried by a king or queen as a symbol of authority

sceptic see skeptic

schadenfreude (German) pleasure felt at the misfortune of another

schema an underlying structure or framework; outline

schism a separation into opposing groups

schmooze to chat idly

scholar a person of great learning

scintilla the slightest amount

scintillate to give off sparks; to be exciting or brilliant

scion a descendant or offspring, esp. of a prominent family

sclerotic grown rigid or unresponsive, as a bureaucracy

scoff to criticize mockingly

scope limits or range

scorn a strong feeling of contempt

scotch to put an end to, as a rumor

scoundrel a villainous, dishonorable person

scourge a cause of widespread suffering

screed a lengthy piece of writing, esp. a severe criticism

scrimmage a vigorous struggle

scrimp   to be frugal or stingy

scrofulous   diseased; morally contaminated

scruples   moral or ethical considerations

scrupulous   extremely attentive to details; ethical

scrum   a place of confusion and racket

scrumptious   delicious

scrutable   capable of being understood or deciphered

scrutinize   to examine closely

scrutiny   close observation

scullion   a kitchen servant

scurrilous   containing coarse and abusive language

scurvy   a disease of body tissues caused by a lack of vitamin C

scuttle   to sink a ship by making holes in it; to discard or abandon something

seamy   low and disagreeable

seance   a meeting in which people attempt to communicate with the dead

seasonable   suitable to the time of year

secede   to withdraw formally from an alliance

seclusion   withdrawal from human contact; isolation

secrete   (of a cell or gland) to produce and release a liquid; to conceal in a hiding place

sectarian   narrowly limited in character or scope

secular   not related to religion; worldly

sedate   calm and dignified

sedentary   involving little physical activity; accustomed to taking little exercise

sedition   incitement of rebellion against a government

seduce   to induce to have sex; to persuade to engage in wrongful behavior

sedulous   persistent in character or application; persevering

seemingly in a way that appears to be so but may not be; apparently

seemly sociably suitable and proper

seethe to be in an agitated state

segregate to separate a group from the rest of society, as because of race

segue (SEG.way) to make a smooth transition from one topic to another

seismic pertaining to or caused by an earthquake

seizure a sudden fit or convulsion, as in epilepsy

select carefully chosen; choice

self-abnegation self-sacrifice; self-denial

self-denial the practice of restraining one's desires

self-effacing humble; modest

selfless unselfish

selfsame being the very same; identical

semantics a branch of linguistics that deals with the study of meaning

semblance outward appearance; actual or apparent resemblance

semiannual occurring or published twice a year

semimonthly occurring or published twice a month

seminal containing important new ideas that influence later development

seminar a short course or special meeting on a particular subject

semiotics the study of signs and symbols as elements of communication

Semitic relating to the Arabs and Jews of the Middle East

semper fidelis always faithful: motto of the U.S. Marine Corps

senescent growing old; aging

senile showing a deterioration of mental ability as a result of old age

sensate relating to or experienced through the senses

sensual related to sexual pleasure

sensuous giving pleasure through the senses

sententious given to excessive moralizing; self-righteous

sentient able to experience perception by the senses; conscious

sentinel a person or thing that stands watch

septic relating to or caused by bacteria or their toxins in the bloodstream

septuagenarian a person who is between 70 and 80 years old

sepulcher a burial tomb

sepulchral pertaining to tombs or burial; (of tones) hollow and deep

sequellae abnormal conditions resulting from a previous disease

sequential following in order

sequester to remove or withdraw to a private place

seraglio a harem

sere dry; withered

serendipity the aptitude for finding valuable things by chance

serene peaceful; tranquil

serf a laborer who worked the land in feudal times

serial a work of fiction or non-fiction presented in installments

serpentine having many bends or curves

serrated having a notched or sawlike edge

servile acting like a servant; willingly submissive

sexagenarian a person who is between 60 and 70 years old

shaman a wise man who is believed to have magic powers

shamble to walk slowly and awkwardly

shambles a place or condition of great disorder or destruction

sheaf a collection of things bundled

together

sheath a case into which the blade of a knife fits

shear to cut

sheathe to enclose in a case or covering

shibboleth a common belief or custom that has little current meaning or value

shiftless lacking ambition or purpose; lazy

shifty evasive; untrustworthy

shilly-shally to be indecisive

shindig a large party

shoal a sandbank in a body of water, esp. one that is visible at low tide

shortfall an amount that is less than expected or needed

shrapnel small pieces of metal that are scattered by a bursting shell or bomb

shrew a bad-tempered woman

shrewd sharp in practical matters

shunt to move aside or divert to an alternate course

sibilant producing a hissing sound, as the consonant S

sibling a brother or sister

sibyl a female prophet or fortune teller

sidelong directed to one side

sidereal of or calculated by the stars

sideswipe to hit a vehicle along the side in passing

sidetrack to distract from the main issue or course

sidle to move forward in an uncertain or sly manner

siege the surrounding and blockading of a place by an armed force; a prolonged period of illness or difficulty

sieve a kitchen utensil with a meshed surface used for straining liquids

signatory the signer of a document

signet a small official seal for legal documents

signify to represent or mean; to make

known

simian pertaining to or characteristic of an ape or monkey

simile a figure of speech comparing one thing with another

similitude likeness; resemblance

simper to smile in a silly way

simulacrum an image or representation; a slight or superficial likeness

simulate to give the appearance of; to pretend

simplistic overly simplified

simultaneous existing or occurring at the same time

sinecure an office or position that provides an income but requires little or no work

sine qua non something that is absolutely essential

sinew a band of tough tissue that connects a muscle with a bone; strength or power

singular extraordinary; unique; strange

sinister seeming to suggest evil or harm

sinuous having many curves or turns

siphon to draw off or empty

sirocco a hot, oppressive wind that blows from the Sahara Desert to southern Europe

skeptic or **sceptic** a person who doubts the truth or value of an idea or belief

skew to turn or place to one side or at an angle; to distort or misrepresent

skewer a long, thin rod used to hold pieces of meat or vegetables for cooking

skimp to give insufficient attention or effort to; to be frugal or stingy

skirmish a minor fight between small bodies of troops

skittish excitable or nervous

skulduggery dishonest or deceitful behavior

skulk to hide or move about stealthily

slack not tight; not active or busy;

sluggish

slake to satisfy a thirst or desire

slander a false statement about someone that damages their reputation

slather to spread thickly

slattern a dirty, untidy woman; a slut or harlot

slay to kill violently

sleight of hand a trick or set of tricks performed quickly and cleverly

sleuth a detective

slight to treat rudely by ignoring

slipshod done carelessly or badly

slither to move with a sliding motion, as a snake

sloe-eyed having very dark or slanted eyes

slog to make one's way with great effort

sloth lack of ambition; laziness

slough (sloo) a condition of despair

slough (sluff) to cast off; shed

slovenly messy; careless

sluggard a lazy, inactive person

sluggish lazy; slow

sluice an artificial channel for carrying a current of water

slur an insulting or degrading remark

smarmy insincerely flattering or agreeable

smattering a slight or superficial knowledge of something

smidgen a very small amount

smirch to tarnish a reputation

smite to hit forcefully

smitten in love

smut indecent or obscene material

snafu a badly confused situation

snipe to attack with unpleasant criticism, esp. from a distance

snit an irritated mood

snivel to complain in a whining manner

snorkel a breathing device used by skin divers

snub to treat rudely by ignoring

sobriquet   a nickname

socialism   a political system in which the means of production and distribution are controlled by the state

socialite   a person who is prominent in fashionable society

sociopath   a person who lacks a sense of morality or social conscience

sodality   a charitable and devotional society of Roman Catholic laity

sodden   thoroughly soaked

sodomy   anal or oral copulation

soi-disant   self-styled; so-called

soignée   (swah.NYAY)   well-groomed

soiree   (swah.RAY)   an evening party or social gathering

sojourn   a temporary stay

solace   comfort from grief or worry

solder   that which joins or unites

solecism   a nonstandard or ungrammatical usage

solemn   deeply serious; sacred or religious; gloomy

solicitous   concerned and attentive

solidarity   unity of purpose

soliloquy   a speech in a play in which the actor speaks to himself or herself

solipsism   the belief that only the self can be proven to exist; self-absorption

solitude   the state of being alone; seclusion

solstice   either of the two times in the year when the sun is at its greatest distance from the celestial equator

soluble   able to be dissolved in a liquid; able to be solved

somatic   of the body; physical

somber   gloomy; serious

sommelier   a wine steward in a restaurant

somnambulism   walking in one's sleep

somniferous or somnific   causing sleep

somnolent   sleepy; drowsy

sonorous   rich and full in sound

soothsayer a person who foretells future events

sop something of little value that is offered to pacify or bribe

sophisticated worldly-wise or cultivated; elaborate or complex

sophistry the clever use of subtly deceptive reasoning

sophomoric immature and foolish

soporific tending to induce sleep

sordid filthy; shameful

sotto voce (VOH.che) in a low voice so as not to be overheard

soubrette a pert lady's maid in a play or opera

soupçon (soop.SAWN) a slight trace or hint

souse a drunkard

sovereign a king or queen

sparingly scantily; meagerly

sparse scattered over a large area

spasmodic lasting for only short periods of time

spastic afflicted with spasm

spate a large number or amount

spatial relating to space

spawn to produce offspring; to cause or bring about

species (in biology) individuals who resemble each other and are able to breed among themselves, but not with other species

specification a clear, detailed description, as of a product

specious seeming to be true but actually false

specter a ghost; a frightening image or possibility

spectral ghostly

spectrum (pl. **spectra**) a wide range, as of opinions; a range of light waves or radio waves

speculate   to form opinions without the necessary information; to take business or financial risks

sphincter   a band of muscle that surrounds an opening in the body, as the anus

sphinx   an ancient Egyptian figure of an imaginary creature with the body of a lion and the head of a human; a silent, mysterious person

spin   a particular slant or interpretation, esp. in the media

splay   to spread out or expand

spleen   an internal organ that stores and filters the blood; ill humor or anger

splendor   great beauty; magnificence

splenetic   irritable; spiteful

spontaneous   happening in a natural way without being planned or forced

sporadic   happening at irregular intervals

spume   foam; froth

spurious   false

spurn   to reject in an unkind way

spurt   a sudden short burst of activity or effort

sputum   matter coughed up from the lungs

squalid   filthy and wretched; degraded

squalor   a condition of filth and misery

squander   to spend wastefully

squash   to flatten or crush

squelch   to put down or silence

squib   a short, sarcastic piece of writing; a short news story used as a filler

squire   to escort a woman

staccato   consisting of a series of short, separate sounds

squash   to flatten or crush

stagnant   (of water) not moving and foul; inactive or sluggish

stagy or **stagey**   too theatrical; overdone

staid   stiffly proper in manner; reserved

stalemate   a situation in which no further action can be taken; deadlock

stalwart   strong and loyal

stamina   strength or power to endure

stanch or staunch   to stop or slow a flow, esp. of blood

statuesque   (of women) tall and graceful

statute   a written law

statutory   (of an offense) punishable according to written law

staunch   loyal and dedicated

stealth   secret or indirect action

stellar   relating to stars; outstanding or brilliant

stemwinder   a lengthy, rousing speech

stenography   the process of writing in shorthand

stentorian   (of the voice) very loud and powerful

steward   a male attendant on a ship or plane

stewardship   the responsible management of something entrusted to one's care

stigma   a mark of shame or disgrace

stigmata   marks resembling the wounds of the crucified Christ

stigmatize   to mark someone as shameful or disgraceful

stiletto   a short dagger with a narrow blade; a high, narrow heel on a woman's shoe

stilted   stiffly dignified or formal

stimulus   something that causes an action or response

stint   (n) a limited period of time spent on a particular job or activity

stint   (v) to limit to a certain amount or number; to be frugal

stipend   a fixed sum of money paid periodically for services or as a gift

stipulate   to state exactly as a condition of an agreement

stodgy   dull and boring

stoic   seemingly unaffected by emotion or

pain

stolid   showing little feeling; unemotional

straits   a position of great difficulty or need

stratagem   a scheme or trick to gain an advantage

strategic   required for the conduct of war

strategy   a detailed plan of action

stratify   to arrange in separate layers or groups

stratum   (pl. **strata**)   a layer or level, as a level of society composed of people with similar social and economic status

straw man   a weak or invented opposition set up only to be defeated

strenuous   needing great effort; intensely active or energetic

striated   having long thin lines, marks, or strips of color

stricture   a limitation or restriction; a statement of severe criticism or disapproval

strife   bitter disagreement or conflict

stripling   a youth

strident   loud and harsh

striking   very attractive; noticeable

stringent   rigorously binding; severe

stultify   to have a dulling or inhibiting effect

stupefy   to astound or amaze

stupendous   tremendous; amazing

stupor   a state of senselessness; a daze

Stygian   dark and gloomy

stylize   to cause to conform to a particular style

stymie   to stop or block someone or something; to hinder or thwart

suasion   the act of attempting to persuade

suave   (esp. of men) smoothly polite and charming

subaltern   someone lower in rank than another

subcutaneous   existing under the skin

subdue to overpower by superior force; to reduce the intensity of; to bring under control

subdued quiet; controlled

subjective based on personal feelings rather than facts

subjugate to bring under control

sublimate to divert the expression of a strong impulse to one that that is more socially acceptable

sublime excellent; wonderful

subliminal existing below the level of consciousness

submerge to go or put under water

submissive humbly obedient or compliant

submit to yield to a greater power; to present for approval or consideration

subordinate belonging to a lower rank; of lesser importance

subpoena a legal document requiring a person to appear in court

subrogate to put into the place of another

sub rosa secretly; privately

subsequent following in time or order

subservient submissive to the will of others

subside to become less strong or intense

subsidiary (adj) secondary in importance

subsidiary (n) a company whose controlling interest is owned by another company

subsidy direct financial aid paid to a person, group, or business

subsistence a basic level of living or existence

substantial solidly built; of considerable amount or size

substantiate to establish or support with facts or evidence

substantive real; solid

subsume to include within something larger or more comprehensive

subterfuge   a deceitful action taken to conceal or evade something

subterranean   below the earth's surface; underground

subtext   the underlying or less obvious meaning

subtle   difficult to detect; indirect; able to make fine distinctions

subvention   a grant of money, as by a government to support an undertaking

subversive   attempting to overthrow or weaken an established political system

subvert   to undermine or cause the downfall of something

successive   following one after the other

succinct   clear and concise

succor   help given to someone who is suffering

succubus   a demon in female form who has sexual intercourse with men in their sleep

succulent   full of juice; moist and tasty

succumb   to yield to a superior force; to die

sufferance   passive or unwilling permission

suffrage   the right to vote

suffuse   to spread through or over, as with a liquid

suggestible   easily influenced

suggestive   hinting at something improper or indecent

sui generis   of its own kind; unique

sullen   showing resentment by being silent and withdrawn

sully   to stain, as a reputation

sulphurous   pertaining to the fires of hell

sultry   very hot and humid; (of a woman) sexually attractive

summa cum laude   with the highest academic honor

summarily   in a prompt or direct manner; immediately

summation   a summary

summon   to call or send for

sumptuous   grand and expensive; luxurious

sunder   to separate or sever

sundry   various; miscellaneous

superannuated   too old for work or service; obsolete

superb   excellent

supercilious   haughtily superior; snobbish

superego   the part of the mind that represents the conscience

superficial   on the surface only; limited in understanding; shallow

superfluous   more than is required or wanted

superimpose   to place over or above something else

superlative   of the highest order or quality

supernatural   beyond the natural world

supernova   an exploding star that is many times brighter than the sun

supernumerary   an extra person or thing

supersede   to replace in power, effectiveness, or use

supervene   to result as an additional or unexpected development

supine   lying on the back with the face upward

supplant   to take the place of

supple   easily bent; agile

supplement   something added to complete or improve an existing thing

supplicant or **suppliant**   a person who asks for something in a humble manner

supplicate   to make a humble and earnest plea

supposition   a guess or speculation

suppurate   to discharge pus

surcease   a cessation or end

surfeit   an excessive amount

surly   bad-tempered

surmise   to conclude without strong

evidence; to guess or suppose

surmount to overcome

surrealism a 20th-century style of art based on the product of dreams and the unconscious mind

surreptitious done in secret

surrogate a person or thing that takes the place of another

surveillance close observation of a person or group under suspicion

susceptible easily influenced or affected by something

sustain to maintain in existence

sustenance the support of life, as with food

suture a stitch used in surgery

svelte slim and graceful

Svengali a person who completely dominates another, usually with evil intentions

swaddle to wrap an infant tightly in cloth; to restrain or restrict

swain a male admirer or suitor

swami a Hindu religious teacher

swan song a final act or farewell appearance

swarthy having a dark complexion

swashbuckler a daring soldier or adventurer

swath a long strip cut through grass or grain by a scythe or mower

swathe to cover or wrap

sway to influence or control

sweltering extremely hot and humid

swill garbage; refuse

swinish extremely coarse and rude

swoon to faint

sybarite a person who loves luxury and pleasure

sycophant a self-seeking flatterer

syllabus an outline of topics for a course of study

syllogism a process of logic in which a major and minor premise lead to a conclusion

sylph a slender, graceful woman or girl

sylvan related to the woods or forest

symbiosis the living together of two dissimilar organisms

symmetry the orderly and similar distribution of parts; regularity in form and arrangement

synagogue a building for worship and religious instruction in the Jewish faith

synapse a region where electrical signals move from one nerve cell to another

syncope a fainting spell

synchronize to cause to occur at the same rate and time

syndrome a set of symptoms that together characterize a specific disease or disorder

synecdoche a figure of speech in which a part is used for the whole or the whole for a part

synergy combined action or functioning

synod a meeting of church leaders to determine policy

synonym a word having the same or nearly the same meaning as another word

synopsis a brief summary or outline

syntax the grammatical arrangement of words in sentences according to established usage in a language

synthesis the combination of separate elements into a whole

systematic characterized by order and planning

systemic relating to an entire system; affecting the body as a whole

=T=

tabernacle a place of worship

tableau a vivid representation of a scene

table d'hôte a complete meal of preselected courses offered at a fixed price

tabula rasa a blank slate

tabulate to condense and list information

tacit not spoken or written; implied

taciturn inclined to be silent; uncommunicative

tack a different course of action

tactic a plan or procedure for achieving a goal

tactile capable of being felt by touch

taint a trace of scandal or corruption

talisman an object thought to have magical powers

tally (n) a list or score

tally (v) to correspond or agree

tamper to interfere or influence improperly

tandem one behind the other; together

tangent a sudden digression from the main point

tangible able to be felt or understood; real, rather than imaginary

tantalize to tempt with something desired but out of reach

tantamount equivalent, as in force or effect

tare an allowance for the weight of the container for a substance

tariff a tax imposed by a government on imports and exports

tarot any of a set of playing cards used in telling fortunes

tatterdemalion ragged or shabby in appearance

tatty shabby or dilapidated

tautology useless repetition of an idea in different words

tchotchke a small ornamental article or trinket; a knickknack

technocracy management of society and the economy by technological experts

tectonic relating to the forces within the earth that cause movements of the earth's crust

tedium boredom

teetotaler a person who abstains from alcoholic beverages

telegenic having an attractive appearance on television

telekinesis the ability to move objects without physical contact

teleology the philosophical doctrine that everything has a design or purpose

telesis attainment of desired goals through intelligent planning and direction

telling having force and effect

temblor an earthquake

temerity reckless boldness

temper to soften or tone down; to moderate

temperamental easily upset or irritated; moody

temperance moderation and self-control; total abstinence from alcoholic liquors

temperate not extreme or excessive; moderate

tempest a violent storm

tempestuous violent and uncontrolled; stormy

template a pattern or guide

temporal relating to worldly affairs as opposed to religious ones

temporize to delay making a decision in order to gain an advantage

tempus fugit time flies

tenable capable of being held or defended,

as a theory

tenacious holding fast; persistent or stubborn

tenancy possession or occupancy, as by lease

tendentious marked by a tendency toward a particular point of view; biased

tenebrous gloomy; obscure

tenet one of the principles on which a belief or theory is based

tenor the thought or meaning running through something written or spoken

tensile capable of being stretched or drawn out

tentative not fully worked out or developed; indefinite

tenterhooks a state of suspense or anxiety

tenuous lacking a sound basis; having little substance

tenure a period during which someone holds a position; the status of holding an academic position on a permanent basis

tepid moderately warm; lukewarm

termagant a bad-tempered, nagging woman

terminate to bring to an end

terminology the system of terms used in a particular field

terminus the station at the end of a railway or bus line

Terpsichore (turp.SICK.o.ree) the art of dancing; the Greek muse of the dance

terra firma solid ground; dry land

terra incognita unknown land

terrestrial related to or coming from the planet earth

terse brief and to the point

tertiary of the third order or rank

testament something that serves as proof; a statement of belief; a will

tête-à-tête a private conversation between two people

tether a restraint, such as a rope or leash

thanatopsis a contemplation of death

theism belief in one God as the creator of the universe

thence from there on

thenceforth from that time onward

theocentric centered on God

theocracy a form of government in which God is recognized as the supreme ruler

theology the study of religion and the nature of religious truth

theorem a mathematical proposition that can be shown to be true by reasoning

theoretical not proven

theorize to form a theory

theosophy religious philosophy based on mystical insight into the nature of God

therapeutic used for healing or curing

therapy the treatment of disease or disorders, as by medication or rehabilitation

theretofore up to that time

thereupon immediately following that

thermal relating to heat

thermodynamics the area of physics that deals with the relationship between heat and mechanical energy

thermonuclear relating to reactions caused by the fusion of nuclei at high temperatures

thesis a formal paper resulting from original research; an argument or theory

thither to or toward that place

thoroughfare a main road or public highway

thoroughgoing carried out to the full extent; complete

thrall a state of servitude or submission

thrice three times

throes pains or spasms; a hard and painful struggle

throng a very large group of people

crowded together

thwart to block or prevent

till (n) a drawer where money is kept in a store

till (v) to plow the land

timbre the particular quality of tone of a singing voice or musical instrument

timorous fearful; timid

tincture an alcohol solution of a medication

tinder any dry, easily ignitable material used to start fires

tinge a slight amount of color; a hint of something

tipple to drink liquor to excess

tipsy slightly drunk

tirade a long, angrily critical speech

tithe a tenth of one's income given to a church or charity

titillate to excite or stimulate

titular being such in title only

toady a self-serving flatterer

toff a well-dressed, stylish person who aspires to the upper class

tome a large, heavy book

tonsorial pertaining to a barber

tonsure cutting of the hair or shaving the head

tony high-toned; stylish

toothsome delicious; alluring

topical dealing with matters of current interest; designed for local application on the body

topography the physical features of an area, such as mountains and valleys

torpid inactive and dull; sluggish

torpor inactivity due to indifference or lack of energy

torque a force that causes twisting or rotation

torrent a heavy outpouring, as of criticism; heavy rain

torrid very dry and hot; passionate

torsion the act of twisting

tort a wrongful act that causes another person harm or damage

tortuous full of twists and turns

torturous causing suffering

tosspot a drunkard

totalitarian relating to a form of government that exercises dictatorial control over its people

totality the total amount; a whole

totem an animal, plant, or object serving as the symbol of a group of people

touché an expression used to indicate that someone has made a good point in an argument or discussion; a point in fencing

touchstone a test or standard by which something is judged

tour de force a masterly or brilliant feat

tourniquet something used to stop the flow of blood in a limb, as a bandage that is tightened by twisting

tousled (of the hair) rumpled or disheveled

tout (n) a person who gives information on a racehorse for a fee

tout (v) to promote or publicize energetically

toute de suite (toot SWEET) at once; immediately

tractable easily managed or controlled

traduce to slander or defame

traipse to walk aimlessly or idly

trajectory the curved path of a moving body in flight

trammel a hindrance or restraint

tranquil peaceful; calm

transact to conduct business

transcend to go above or beyond the ordinary limits

transcribe to make a written or typed copy, as of dictated material

transfigure to change in outward form or appearance, as in a spiritual way

transfix to hold motionless, as in awe or amazement

transfuse to transfer blood into a vein; to permeate or diffuse

transgress to act in violation of a law or moral code

transient lasting or staying in one place only a short time

transitory lasting for only a short time; short-lived

translate to turn from one language into another; to convert into a different form

translucent allowing light to pass through; easily understandable

transmit to pass from one to another; to broadcast

transmogrify to change in appearance or form, esp. in a strange way

transmute to change from one substance, form, or condition into another

transpire to happen; to become known

transplant to move from one place or person to another

transport to carry from one place to another

transpose to reverse the order, as of letters in a word

transsexual a person who assumes the gender role and physical characteristics of the opposite sex

transubstantiation the changing of one substance into another, as in the Eucharist

transverse lying or extending across

transvestite a person who wears the clothing of the opposite sex

trappings articles of equipment or dress characteristic of a particular job or situation

trauma a serious injury or emotional

shock that causes lasting damage

traumatic   shocking; harmful

travails   painful or burdensome difficulties

traverse   to go across, over, or through

travesty   a mocking or debased likeness of something

treachery   betrayal of trust

treacle   something that is excessively sweet or sentimental

treatise   a formal piece of writing that examines a particular subject

tremor   an involuntary shaking of the body or limbs; a shaking of the earth

tremulous   trembling; fearful

trenchant   keen and cutting

trencherman   a man who has a hearty appetite

trepidation   a state of anxiety or fear; apprehension

triage   the process of sorting victims for treatment according to urgency

tribulation   great suffering or distress

tribunal   a court of justice

tribune   a person who defends the rights of the people

trice   a very short time; an instant

trident   a three-pronged spear, esp. that of the sea god Poseidon

trilogy   a series of three books or plays forming a continuous story

tripartite   consisting of three parts

tripe   writing or ideas that have no value; rubbish

trite   lacking freshness or originality because of overuse

triumvirate   a board or government of three officials

trivial   of little importance or value

troglodyte   a person of primitive, brutal character

trollop   a prostitute

trompe l'oeil   (tromp loy)   visual deception

in painting

trope a figure of speech

troth one's word or promise

trounce to defeat decisively

troupe a company or group of performers

trouper a loyal and dependable worker

trove a valuable collection of objects

truant a pupil who is absent without permission

truculent aggressively hostile; belligerent

truism a self-evident truth

trump to excel or surpass

trumped-up devised deceitfully, as an accusation; fabricated

trumpery something without use or value

truncated cut short

truncheon a heavy club used as a weapon

trundle to move something along slowly on wheels

tryptich a painting or carving in three panels side by side

tryst a secret meeting between lovers

tsunami a tidal wave

tumescent swollen

tumult the noise made by an excited crowd; confusion of the mind or emotions

tumultuous noisy and disorderly

tundra a vast, trecless plain of Arctic regions

turbid muddy; cloudy

turbulent being in a state of violent agitation or disorder

turgid swollen or bloated; (of prose) complex and boring

turpitude vile or depraved character

tutelage instruction or guidance

tweak to make a minor adjustment

twit (n) a foolish and annoying person

twit (v) to taunt or ridicule

tyranny absolute power exercised unjustly

tyro a beginner or novice

=U=

Übermensch (German) superman

ubiquitous seeming to be everywhere at the same time

ufology the study of unidentified flying objects

ulterior intentionally kept hidden

ultimate last or final; greatest possible; basic or fundamental

ultimatum a final, uncompromising demand

ultrasonic relating to sound waves that are above the upper limit of human hearing

ultrasound the medical use of ultrasonic waves in therapy and diagnosis

ululate to howl or wail, esp. employing the tongue

umbilicus the navel

umbrage offense; resentment

unabashed not embarrassed or concerned

unabated with undiminished force; without stopping

unaccountable impossible to explain

unadulterated pure; thorough

unaffected sincere; genuine

unalloyed unmixed; pure

unalterable impossible to change

unanimity complete agreement

unassailable not subject to denial or dispute

unassuming modest; unpretentious

unbeknown or **unbeknownst** without one's knowledge; unknown

unbiased without bias or prejudice; impartial

unbounded having no limits; unrestrained

unbowed not yielding to defeat

unbridled not restrained; uninhibited

uncanny so extraordinary as to seem

supernatural

unceremonious without formalities; hasty or rude

unchaste impure

unconscionable without a conscience; unethical; immoral

uncouth ill-mannered; crude

unction the act of anointing, as in a religious rite

unctuous marked by a false earnestness and smooth manner

undaunted not discouraged; courageous

undergraduate a college student who has not yet received a degree

underhanded secret and crafty

underlie to be the basis for

underling an unimportant subordinate

undermine to weaken or ruin

undermost lowest in position or status

underpinnings the foundation or basis

underplay to play down or deemphasize

undertake to take upon oneself, as a task

undertone an implied meaning

underwhelm to fail to interest or impress

underwrite to assume financial responsibility for

undone brought to destruction or ruin

undue excessive; inappropriate

undulate to move in a wavy motion

unduly excessively; unjustifiably

unequivocal having only one possible interpretation; without any doubt

unerring without error; consistently accurate

unfathomable impossible to understand

unfettered not restricted or restrained

unflagging never weakening

unflappable not easily upset or confused; calm under pressure

unfurl to unroll, as a flag

ungainly clumsy; awkward

unguent a healing salve or ointment

ungulate   belonging to the order of hoofed mammals

unilateral   relating to or occurring on one side only

unimpeachable   beyond doubt or question

uninhibited   not restrained by social conventions

unionize   to organize workers into a labor union

unique   having no like or equal; being the only one of its kind

unisex   suitable to both sexes

unison   agreement; harmony

unlettered   uneducated; ignorant

unmitigated   not lessened or softened; absolute

unnerve   to deprive of courage or confidence; to upset

unobtrusive   not easily noticed; inconspicuous

unpalatable   unpleasant to the taste; disagreeable or unacceptable

unparalleled   exceptional; unequaled

unprecedented   never before known or experienced

unpretentious   modest

unquiet   agitated; restless

unrelenting   without stopping; persistent

unremitting   not abating; incessant

unrepentant   showing no regret for past wrongs

unrequited   not returned equally

unruffled   calm

unsavory   distasteful; offensive

unscathed   not harmed or injured

unscrupulous   without principles; dishonest

unseemly   not in good taste; inappropriate

unspeakable   shockingly bad beyond description

unstinting   given freely or generously

unstrung   nervously upset

unsubstantial   having no basis in fact

unsullied   untarnished

untenable   not capable of being defended, as a thesis

untoward   unfavorable; improper

untrammeled   not limited by rules or controls

unutterable   beyond expression; unspeakable

unwary   not cautious or watchful; unsuspecting

unwarranted   not needed or deserved

unwieldy   hard to handle or manage in use because of shape or size

unwitting   unaware; not intended

unwonted   not customary or usual; rare

upbraid   to criticize severely

upload   to transfer data from a smaller to a larger computer

uppity   haughty; snobbish

upscale   relating or appealing to affluent consumers

upshot   final result; outcome

upstage   to behave snobbishly toward; to take attention or praise away from

upstart   an arrogant person who has risen suddenly to wealth or importance

upsurge   a large or rapid rise or increase

uptake   mental grasp; comprehension

uptick   a sharp rise in the stock market

upturn   an upward trend, as in business

urban   related to a city

urbane   having worldly knowledge and refined manners

urchin   a mischievous boy, often living in poverty

urologist   a physician who specializes in the urinary and genitourinary tract

ursine   pertaining to bears; bearlike

usurp   to seize control of the rights, property, or role of another

usury   the practice of lending money at an

excessively high rate of interest

utensil   a tool or implement, esp. for eating food

utilitarian   useful; practical

utilize   to put to use

utmost or **uttermost**   of the highest or greatest degree

utopia   a visionary place of ideal perfection

utter   complete; absolute

utterance   something expressed; a statement

utterly   completely; absolutely

uvula   the small fleshy body that hangs down from the end of the soft palate

uxorious   excessively fond of or submissive to one's wife

=V=

vacillate to waver between two courses of action; to hesitate

vacuous empty; stupid

vagary a whimsical or unpredictable action or notion

vagrant a person who wanders about and has no permanent home or job

vague not clearly expressed or felt

vain unsuccessful or useless; excessively proud of one's appearance or accomplishments

vainglorious excessively proud of one's achievements; boastful

valedictory a closing speech delivered at a graduation ceremony

valiant courageous; brave

valid based on truth or reason; convincing; legal

validate to make officially acceptable or approved; to establish the truth

valor boldness and courage in the face of danger

vamp a seductive woman who exploits men

vanguard the leading position in a trend or movement

vanity conceit

vanquish to defeat or conquer

vantage a position that allows a commanding view

vapid lacking spirit or interest; empty and dull

variable changeable

variance an exception to a rule or standard

variegated marked with streaks of different colors

various of several different kinds; assorted

varsity the main team representing a school or college

vary to modify or alter; to be different from others of its type

vassal a servant or slave

vaunt to boast of one's achievements

vector the direction or course of a moving object; something or someone that carries and transmits a disease-causing organism

veer to turn aside from a course or purpose

vegetate to be physically, mentally, and socially inactive

vehement fierce; forceful; very angry

vehicle a means of expressing something

vein an attitude or mood; a blood vessel through which blood returns to the heart and lungs

velocity speed; swiftness

velour a soft fabric resembling velvet

venal corrupt; dishonest

vendetta a prolonged and bitter feud

vendor or **vender** a person who sells something

vengeance bitter retaliation for a wrong

veneer a false outer appearance

venerable worthy of respect because of age or high position

venerate to regard with respect or reverence

venial able to be forgiven or pardoned; minor

venom a poisonous substance produced by certain snakes; anger or hatred

venomous angry; hateful

vent to give free expression to an emotion

ventilate to expose an opinion or complaint to public discussion

venture an undertaking, such as a business enterprise, involving risk or uncertainty

venturesome or **venturous** adventurous; daring

venue   the setting in which something takes place

veracity   truthfulness; honesty

verbatim   corresponding word for word

verbiage   overabundance of words

verbose   using more words than necessary; wordy

verdant   covered with greenery

verge   to border on; approach

verisimilitude   the appearance of truth or reality

veritable   real or genuine

verity   the state of being true; something that is true, as a principle

vermin   small animals or insects that can be harmful and difficult to control

vernacular   the plain, everyday language spoken in a country or region

vernal   pertaining to or occurring in spring

versatile   able to do many things well; having various uses

versify   to put into verse

versus   in opposition to; against

vertebrate   an animal having a spine, as birds, fishes, and mammals

vertical   perpendicular to the horizontal plane

vertiginous   spinning or whirling; liable to cause dizziness

vertigo   a sensation of dizziness

verve   energy and enthusiasm

vespers   a religious service in the late afternoon or evening

vested   held completely and permanently, as a right

vested interest   a strong special interest in something for personal reasons

vestibule   a small entrance hall or lobby

vestige   a small trace of something that once existed

vestments   ceremonial clothes worn by clerics

vestry   a room in a church used as a chapel

veto   to block the passage of a law; to forbid or prohibit

vetted   verified or checked for accuracy or authenticity

vex   to irritate or annoy

vexatious   troublesome; annoying

viable   capable of continuing to live; capable of succeeding

viaduct   a long bridge used to carry a road or railroad over a valley

vibrant   full of life; colorful

vibrato   a pulsing effect produced in vocal or instrumental music

vicar   a priest in charge of a local church

vicarious   felt or understood through the experience of another

vice versa   the same but in the opposite order

vicissitudes   changing phases or conditions of life; ups and downs

victuals   food supplies; provisions

vie   to compete

vigilance   alert watchfulness

vignette   a brief, appealing scene in a play or movie

vigorish   usurious interest on loans charged by organized crime

vile   hateful; disgusting

vilify   to criticize harshly; to defame or slander

vindicate   to clear of blame or doubt; to justify or support

vindictive   having a strong desire for revenge; spiteful

vintage   the year in which a wine is bottled

vintner   a winemaker

virago   an ill-tempered, scolding woman; a shrew

virile   strong and manly

virtual   being such in effect but not in actual fact

virtually almost completely; for the most part

virtuosity a high level of skill or style

virtuoso a person who has special skill or knowledge in a field

virtuous moral; upright

virulent extremely infectious or malignant

visage the face

visceral based on emotional reactions rather than on intellect

viscous having a thick and sticky consistency

visionary a person who has the ability to imagine the future

vista a broad, distant view

vital relating to life; having great importance; energetic

vitiate to impair or weaken

viticulture the cultivation of grapes

vitreous relating to or resembling glass

vitriolic bitterly cruel; scathing

vituperative harshly critical

vivacious full of life; lively

vivid strikingly bright, clear, or realistic

vivify to give life to

vivisection the act of cutting into or dissecting a living animal for medical research

vixen a female fox; an ill-tempered woman

vizier a high official in Muslim countries

vociferous noisy and demanding

vogue current fashion or style

volatile marked by sharp or sudden changes; tending to become violent

volcanic potentially explosive

volition one's free will

voluble characterized by a continuous flow of words; talkative

voluminous containing many pages or books; of great volume or size

voluptuous full and shapely; sensual; sexy

voluptuary a person devoted to luxury and

sensual pleasure

voracious   very hungry; very eager

vortex   a swirling force that acts as a suction; a whirlpool

votary   a devoted worshiper or adherent

vouch   to provide proof or assurance

vouchsafe   to grant or allow as a favor

vox populi   the voice of the people; popular opinion

voyeur   a person who gets pleasure from watching in secret the personal lives of others

vulpine   pertaining to or resembling a fox

vying   competing

=W=

wade to spend a lot of effort getting through something difficult; to walk through shallow water

waffle to speak or write without giving direct information or clear answers

waft to float gently through the air

wag a witty person

waggish full of fun and good humor

waif an abandoned child

waive to give up a right or claim; to postpone

wan unnaturally pale

wane to decrease gradually

wanderlust a strong desire to travel

wangle to get something by persuasion or scheming

wanker (British) a masturbator

wannabe a person who aspires to imitate another's success or fame

wanton unrestrained; wild

warble to sing like a bird

ward a minor placed under the care of a guardian

wares articles for sale

warlock a male witch or sorcerer

warmonger a person who encourages war

warrant (n) an official authorization for legal action, such as an arrest

warrant (v) to call for or justify

warren a crowded tenement or area; a maze of passageways or small rooms

wary watchful; cautious

waspish ill-tempered; testy

wasting gradually reducing the strength and size of the body

wastrel a spendthrift; an idler

waver to be unsteady or uncertain; to be undecided

wax   to increase gradually

waylay   to intercept or attack from ambush

weal   well-being or prosperity

wean   to stop former habits

weather   to pass through; to survive safely

welter   a confused mass; a state of turmoil

wheedle   to persuade by flattery or charm

whelp   (of a dog) to give birth to young

whence   from what place or source

wherewithal   the necessary financial means

whet   to sharpen

whimsical   fanciful and unpredictable

whistle-blower   a person who makes public
  disclosure of another's wrongdoing

whit   a tiny amount

white elephant   a possession that is
  expensive to maintain and difficult to
  dispose of

white slave   a woman who is sold into
  prostitution

whitewash   to cover up or make less of a
  fault or error

whither   to what place; where

whittle   to reduce or eliminate gradually

whodunit   a mystery or detective story

wholesale   on a large scale; extensive

wicca   benevolent witchcraft

widget   any small mechanical device

wield   to have and use power or influence

wiles   beguiling behavior used to attract or
  influence

willful   deliberate or intentional;
  unreasonably stubborn

will-o-the-wisp   a false hope; a delusion

willowy   slim and graceful

willy-nilly   in a disorganized manner

wily   full of clever tricks; cunning

wimp   a weak and timid person

windfall   a sudden unexpected piece of
  good fortune

windward   toward the wind

winnow to separate the valuable from the worthless parts

winsome innocently charming

wiseacre a conceited and insolent person

wistful sadly yearning

withdrawn quiet and shy; remote

wither to dry up; to shrivel

witless stupid; foolish

witticism an amusingly clever remark

wizard a very skilled or clever person

wizened dried up; withered

woe deep unhappiness; misfortune

woebegone marked by sadness; forlorn

wonk a student who studies intensively and has no social life; a politician overly concerned with public policy

wont customary practice

woolgathering daydreaming; absentmindedness

woolly unclear; fuzzy

wordsmith a professional writer

workup a thorough medical examination for diagnostic purposes

world-class ranking among the best in the world

worst-case being the worst result possible

wrack damage or destruction

wraith a pale, transparent image of a dead person

wrangle to argue noisily

wrath violent anger

wreak (reck) to do violence

wrench a sharp, distressing surge of emotion

wrest to gain or take away forcefully

wretched very unhappy or unfortunate

wring to twist or squeeze

writ a written court order

writhe to twist, as in pain

wrought-up upset; disturbed

wry humorous in a dry or ironic manner; distorted or lopsided

=X=

xenograft   a graft from one species that is transplanted into a member of another species

xenophile   a person who is attracted to foreigners and their culture

xenophobia   an unreasonable fear and dislike of foreigners

xerography   a process for producing photocopies

xylophone   a musical instrument consisting of two rows of wooden bars that produce various tones when struck with two small mallets

=Y=

yahoo an uneducated, boorish person

Yahweh a name for God

yakuza a Japanese crime syndicate

yammer to whine or complain continuously

yap to talk in a shrill and foolish manner; to bark sharply

yarmulke a skullcap worn by religious male Jews

yaw (of a ship) to deviate temporarily from a straight course

yearling an animal that is one year old

yearn to long for

yenta a gossipy busybody

yeoman a naval petty officer; a dependable worker

yeomanly sturdy and dependable

yeshiva an Orthodox Jewish rabbinical seminary

Yiddish a language derived from German and spoken by Jews of European origin

yield to give over possession of; to give up, as in defeat

yin and yang the feminine and masculine principles in Chinese philosophy

yippie a member of a group of politically radical young people

yoga a system of exercises for attaining control of the body and mind

yoke the condition of being dominated by a tyrant

yokel a simple country person

yon there; yonder

yonder over there

yoni a representation of the female genitalia in Hindu cosmology

yore time long past

yo-yo to shift back and forth repeatedly

between positions
yuppie a young urban professional who has
an affluent lifestyle

=Z=

zaftig   (of a woman) pleasingly plump

zeal   great enthusiasm, as for a cause

zealot   a person who is excessively devoted to a cause; a fanatic

zealous   eagerly enthusiastic and devoted

Zeitgeist   (German) the spirit of the time; the general set of ideas and feelings characteristic of a particular period in history

Zen   a form of Buddhism that aims at enlightenment through meditation

zenith   the highest point

zephyr   a gentle breeze

zero-sum   relating to a game in which a gain for one side entails a corresponding loss for the other

Zionism   an international movement for the support of Israel

zodiac   (in astrology) a circular representation of the sky divided into the twelve celestial paths of the sun, moon, and planets

zombie   a person who acts like the walking dead, esp. from fatigue

zonked   stupefied by alcohol or drugs; exhausted or asleep

zoology   the scientific study of animals